FLORIDA PROHIBITION

FLORIDA PROHIBITION

CORRUPTION, DEFIANCE & TRAGEDY

RANDY JAYE

Published by The History Press
Charleston, SC
www.historypress.com

Front cover, top left: Destruction of a still in Miami, circa 1925. *Courtesy of State Archives of Florida*; *center*: Moonshine still and its accessories discovered in a house attic in Tampa, Florida, circa 1925. *Courtesy of State Archives of Florida*; *top right*: Police destroying confiscated liquor in Miami, Florida, circa 1925. *Courtesy of State Archives of Florida.*
Back cover: "Prohibition Has Sent Many a Fine Man to the Jug—Ye Village Jug." Postcard circa 1925. *Author's collection.*

First published 2024

Manufactured in the United States

ISBN 9781467155823

Library of Congress Control Number: 2023946830

CONTENTS

ACKNOWLEDGEMENTS

Several organizations and people were instrumental in making this book possible, including the Flagler County Historical Society, the Halifax Historical Museum, the State Archives of Florida, David Churchman and Linda Manley.

The Flagler County Historical Society allowed me access to their document archives and historic photographs. The information I was able to retrieve was helpful in understanding how small towns and rural communities in Florida dealt with the perils of Prohibition.

The Halifax Historical Museum allowed me access to their Bill McCoy files, which were very helpful in understanding the life and times of the infamous rumrunner. This organization also allowed me to photograph many of their Bill McCoy artifacts, several of which appear in this book.

Public online access to the central repository for the records of Florida state government, provided by the State Archives of Florida, supplied pertinent information about Prohibition in Florida. Several public domain photographs originating from the State Archives of Florida appear in this book.

One of my former California State University professors, David Churchman, provided some manuscript reviewing and offered various suggestions.

Last but certainly not least, Linda Manley offered support and accompanied me on many information-gathering and photographic adventures that were critical to the completion of this book.

All of which I surely appreciate.

INTRODUCTION

Prohibition was the nationwide constitutional law that prohibited the importation, production, transportation and sale of alcoholic beverages. It was in effect in the United States from 1920 to 1933. Prohibition was intended to eradicate the evils of alcoholism that were negatively affecting millions of people and devastating thousands of families.

In actuality, Prohibition put democracy on trial, as it legally forced people to give up personal freedoms.

Prohibition did not sneak up on the United States; it was brewing (pardon the pun) for many decades before the Eighteenth Amendment to the U.S. Constitution became the law of the land. The temperance movement is a social movement that promotes the temperance or complete abstinence (teetotalism) from the consumption of alcoholic beverages. It actually began in colonial times. In the early 1700s, Native American temperance advocates attempted to restrict the sale and distribution of alcoholic beverages to Indigenous peoples, as they believed alcohol was causing poverty and negative cultural changes. The temperance movement became a significant national social movement from the 1860s into the early 1900s. It was led by evangelical reformers (many Protestant religious groups) among the middle classes who lived mostly in rural areas.

A key factor leading up to Prohibition was anti-immigrant sentiment due to record-high levels of immigration. Between 1882 and 1914, approximately twenty million immigrants entered the United States. Saloons in immigrant communities were major targets for temperance movement activists. Two of the largest and most important temperance organizations were the Woman's Christian Temperance Union and the Anti-Saloon League.

Before the Eighteenth Amendment was ratified in 1919, Florida and many other states had already passed statewide prohibition laws. Florida, similar to most other states, was experiencing significant problems with alcoholism during the nineteenth century. Most women, and many community leaders, wanted to see less alcoholism and better social behavior.

An example of how one community used a local church to deal with alcoholism was the Yellow River Baptist Church in Oak Grove, Okaloosa County. In 1859, the church issued a resolution against what it called the excessive use of "ardent spirits." This was a religious and community persuasion technique to stop a member who was identified as abusing alcoholic beverages from drinking. This was considered living outside the covenant of the church, so a committee, usually three male members, would meet with the abuser of alcohol and pray for them to stop. If the abuser of alcohol would agree to stop, they would be forgiven in the eyes of the church. If not, the abuser of alcohol would be excommunicated from the church.

Nationwide Prohibition attempted to regulate people's behavior. Instead, it instigated corruption and defiance and was the catalyst for many tragedies. It was one of the most tumultuous periods in U.S. history.

Prohibition provided financial opportunities for many illicit and dangerous activities to arise or expand, including bootlegging (the illicit production, selling and smuggling of alcoholic beverages over land), moonshining (the illicit production of high-proof distilled alcoholic beverages) and rumrunning (the illicit transportation and smuggling of alcoholic beverages over water). Prohibition corrupted many people in government and law enforcement and made many criminals large profits.

Prohibition challenged diplomatic relationships between the United States and many of its allies, as many governments were not inclined to enforce its laws. This was especially apparent with Great Britain, as that nation allowed its Caribbean colonies to engage in smuggling liquor into the United States. Many Caribbean Islands, especially the Bahamas, made huge profits via smuggling activities during Prohibition.

During Florida's long history—the oldest European-influenced history in the United States, which started in 1513—Prohibition was one of its most turbulent periods. Florida's proximity to the Caribbean islands and its vast coastline coupled with numerous bays and inlets made it a haven

"Nothing so needs reforming as other people's habits. Fanatics will never learn that, though it be written in letters of gold across the sky. It is the prohibition that makes anything precious."
–Mark Twain

for rumrunning and bootlegging. Thousands of the state's citizens, most of whom were habitually law-abiding, turned into lawbreakers as they ignored Prohibition laws and drank illicit alcoholic beverages and engaged in bootlegging, moonshining and rumrunning.

During Prohibition, Florida was known as a "wet" state because of its easy access to illicit liquor. Since Prohibition was a source of tax-free revenue, many local officials ignored illicit activities, and some accepted bribes that allowed criminals to operate without interference from law enforcement. Florida courts were flooded with cases involving violations of Prohibition laws. The unpopularity of Prohibition prompted many judges to impose low fines and short prison sentences. After being arrested and appearing in court, many lawbreakers quickly returned to working at their illicit trade.

One of the most famous characters in Florida's Prohibition history was rumrunner Bill McCoy, who gained the moniker of the "Real McCoy." McCoy was not alone when it came to colorful characters who were tagged with interesting monikers in Florida's Prohibition history. Several others, including the "Queen of Rum Row," the "Whiskey King of Jacksonville," the "Queen of the Bahamas," "Spanish Marie," the "King of the Florida Smugglers," the "Gulf Stream Pirate," "Miami's Bootleg King," the "Swamp Bandit" and "Pistol Pete," all add mystique and intrigue to the Prohibition era in Florida. Florida's Bill McCoy is credited with the founding of Rum Row. He made the U.S. Coast Guard appear foolish for several years as he avoided capture while making boatloads of money from his rumrunning operations. McCoy was only one of the many rumrunners from Florida, as its vast coastline and proximity to the Caribbean islands made it ideal for smuggling over the high seas.

Defiance of Prohibition laws and corruption led to many violent encounters with law enforcement. Crooks battling crooks were also a cause for many tragedies.

Al Capone, the most infamous gangster in U.S. history, was a frequent visitor to Florida during Prohibition. In fact, he purchased a house in the Miami area and became a part-time resident of the state. Although his notoriety brought money into the state, his mere presence put communities in danger of mob violence. He often did not feel welcome in Florida, as he had frequent encounters with local law enforcement. Capone used his Miami residence as an alibi while he masterminded the St. Valentine's Day Massacre.

Law enforcement of Prohibition in Florida did not treat lawbreakers equally. Many immigrants, Black, poor and working-class people were targeted, as they were easy prey and typically did not have the resources to defend themselves in the courts.

Some bootleggers during Prohibition modified automobiles so they could outrun the police. Many of these bootleggers later became race car drivers and were instrumental in the creation of the National Association for Stock Car Auto Racing (NASCAR).

Florida was the scene of many tragic and violent Prohibition-related murders involving shootouts, ambushes, knifings and lynchings.

When the Great Depression started in 1929, the nation's unemployment soared, and many people became desperate for food, shelter and clothing. The repeal of Prohibition meant that tens of thousands of jobs in the alcohol industry would immediately be created. Millions of dollars of tax revenue to the struggling federal, state and local governments would also be collected. The economic crisis of the Great Depression was a driving factor that persuaded many people to turn against Prohibition.

When national Prohibition was repealed in 1933, Florida stayed dry due to statewide prohibition. Eventually, most counties in Florida became wet, but many taxes on alcoholic beverages, some of the highest in the United States, and many restrictions on the sales of liquor remain in place.

Prohibition in the United States bred hypocrisy and certainly blurred good from evil, illegal from legal and especially right from wrong.

Chapter 1

THE AGE-OLD HUMAN RELATIONSHIP WITH ALCOHOL

Natural fermentation is the process through which microorganisms including yeast and bacteria convert carbohydrates such as starch and sugar into alcohol. Practically all substances that contain sugar, including apples, grapes, oranges, peaches, pears, potatoes and rice, can undergo natural fermentation. So it is not surprising that hunter-gatherers learned long before the dawn of civilization about fermentation and the effects of consuming alcohol.

The consumption of alcohol causes various reactions in the human body by releasing endorphins, which can cause feelings of relaxation, intense excitement, happiness, aggression and depression. It has a love-hate reputation in many societies. Excessive alcohol consumption has intoxicating, mind-altering and many harmful effects, including aggression and learning and memory problems. A long list of health problems linked to alcohol consumption includes various types of cancer, digestive problems, heart disease, liver disease, stroke and weakening of the immune system. This has caused controversy within some societies and turned many people against the use of alcohol. However, throughout the ages, humans have persisted in its use, especially in social contexts, where it has played a key role in communal bonding in many societies.

The archaeological record indicates that humans have been consuming prepared alcohol for at least thirteen thousand years.

Beer

Beer is an alcoholic beverage that is produced from yeast-fermented malt flavored mostly with hops. Evidence of beer production is found all over the world in the earliest of human settlements. Some archaeologists have speculated that the human quest to produce beer was instrumental in the development of agriculture and the formation of ancient civilizations.

Excavations at the Raqefet Cave in the Carmel Mountains near Haifa in Israel provide evidence of residues of beer (one of the oldest intentionally prepared alcoholic drinks in the world). This early beer had the consistency of gruel (a food consisting of some type of cereal including ground oats, rice, rye or wheat that was heated or boiled in water or milk). It was most likely consumed during rituals by the Natufians (a Mesolithic-era culture of semi-sedentary people who thrived in the Mediterranean area before the introduction of agriculture).

Göbekli Tepe, a pre-pottery Neolithic site in modern-day Turkey that dates to around 12,500 years ago, is identified as the oldest-known permanent human settlement anywhere in the world. Archaeologists have analyzed stone vats that they believe were used to grind wild grains to produce porridge and ceremonial beer.

In ancient China, around nine thousand years ago, a type of beer called Lao Li was produced from rice, honey, grapes and hawthorn fruits. It was important in worship, funerals and other rituals during the Xia, Shang and Zhou dynasties.

The Sumerian civilization in southern Mesopotamia (modern-day Iraq) dates to around 6,500 to 3,900 years ago. Sumerian writing, known as the oldest form of writing in the world, came into existence around 5,500 years ago. Ancient Sumerian texts, recorded on clay tablets, describe how their society used beer as a currency system. In the Sumerian city of Uruk, beer was used to trade for precious stones, timber and metal and as a method to pay for labor. Beer was an important factor in the development of the economic structure of this ancient civilization.

Godin Tepe, an archaeological site in western Iran that was an outpost in the early Mesopotamian trade networks, provides similar evidence of beer production using barley dating from 5,500 to 5,100 years ago.

Ancient Egypt is often credited as the producer of the "first beer" because it was made similarly to modern-day brewing techniques. The Egyptians changed Sumerian brewing methods as far back as five thousand years ago to create a lighter beer that could be consumed from

Top: A wooden model of workers making beer in ancient Egypt, circa 2500 BC. Exhibited at Rosicrucian Egyptian Museum, San Jose, California. *Courtesy of Wikimedia Commons.*

Bottom: A drawing from the Mesoamerican Florentine Codex shows Mayahuel, goddess of the maguey, with a mature agave and a pot of fermented *pulque*, circa 1530. *Courtesy of Wikimedia Commons.*

CHRISTOPHER COLUMBUS'S ALCOHOL STASH

When Christopher Columbus made his historic voyages to the West Indies, his cargo included plenty of wine. In 1498, on his third voyage to the New World, the cargo on his Spanish ship *La Niña* included 31 pipes of wine (3,906 U.S. gallons).

cups. In ancient Egypt, everyone from the pharaohs to the common laborers drank beer, which was popular at religious festivals and state and family occasions. During the construction of the Great Pyramid complex, workers were given a large daily ration of beer for nutritional purposes and as a refreshment.

Records in ancient India dating from 4,500 to 3,600 years ago document the production of beer made from rice or millet. Sura, a strong beer-like alcoholic drink that originated around 3,500 years ago, was used in ceremonial practices and as an anesthetic for medical purposes for millennia in the Indian subcontinent.

Germanic and Celtic tribes began making a beer-like drink about 5,000 years ago. This early European beer contained fruits, honey and narcotic herbs. About 1,200 years ago, hops were introduced to beer production in Europe.

Mesoamerican civilizations began around 3,500 years ago. The Aztecs, Huastecs and Mayans produced a beer-like alcoholic drink called *pulque*. It was made from fermented juice or sap from the maguey plant. Pulque is low in alcohol in its raw form, so its potency was often increased by adding various roots and herbs. Evidence from the analysis of pottery in the lower Ulúa Valley in northern Honduras suggests that cacao (the seed from which cocoa and chocolate are made) was most likely prepared as a fermented beer starting about 2,100 years ago.

WINE

Wine is an alcoholic beverage that is typically produced from fermented grapes.

The first evidence of wine production has been traced to the South Caucasus (present-day Armenia, Georgia and Azerbaijan) about nine thousand years ago. Grape juice was stored in large terra-cotta jugs and buried underground during the winter. By the time spring arrived, the grape juice had fermented into wine.

During the Age of Sail (from around 1450 to around 1850), the life of the common sailor was harsh and dangerous. Seamen's diets generally included salted beef and pork, dried peas, beans and oatmeal. Fresh water was stored in wood barrels and oftentimes soured and went bad during the voyages. Alcoholic beverages were actually healthier than the available water. Ships during this era usually carried large quantities of wine and other alcoholic beverages.

Liquor

Liquor is a distilled alcoholic beverage that is purified by undergoing heating and condensation. Types include brandy, whiskey, rum and vodka. Liquor has a much higher alcohol content than fermented beer or wine.

In the eighth century AD, the Arabs developed a pot still that enabled the effective distillation of alcohol.

Brandy originated in France around 1310 as a medicine that was known as "the water of life." Whiskey originated in Scotland around 1494. Rum originated in Caribbean sugarcane plantations in the early 1600s. The origin of vodka is debated; however, its first written record is from Poland in 1405, when it was used as a medicine and a cleanser.

Ethanol and Methanol (Wood Alcohol)

The type of alcohol that humans drink is ethanol, which is the product of the fermentation of simple sugars by yeast. Ethanol can then be distilled to increase its purity and strength. A simpler form of alcohol is methanol, which is quite toxic to humans even in small amounts. Methanol does not occur in the normal fermentation or distillation processes; however, there are some extremely small trace amounts that are not harmful to consume. Methanol was once known as wood alcohol because it was produced through the destructive distillation of wood.

Influence of Alcoholic Beverages in the New World

Before the Spanish Europeans arrived in Florida in 1513, Indigenous tribes including the Apalachee, Calusa, Mayaimi, Ocale, Pensacola, Tequesta, Timucua and Tocobaga did not consume alcoholic beverages. Only the Indigenous peoples living in the present-day southwestern United States consumed alcohol and only for specific rituals. The Pimas and Pagagos tribes used the juice of the saguaro cactus to make an alcoholic drink. They believed that the amount of alcoholic drink consumed in a year determined the amount of rain they would receive. Since they lived in an arid region, they often consumed the alcoholic drink until they became drunk.

European influence and colonization in the New World increased the alcohol consumption patterns of the Indigenous peoples as it became more widespread and was no longer confined to ritual ceremonies. European immigrants imported a culture to the New World that believed alcohol was a gift to human society. They drank alcoholic beverages at most meals, used it to treat various illnesses and celebrated virtually all occasions with it, including christenings, public trials, weddings and even funerals.

European fur traders using a barrel of rum to barter for furs with Native Americans, circa 1777. *Courtesy of Wikimedia Commons.*

Many Americans approved of drinking alcohol in moderation because they believed it was healthy for everyone. However, most condemned its abuse and were concerned with drunkenness and the problems it caused to health, families, communities and society.

Chapter 2

THE TEMPERANCE MOVEMENT BEFORE THE EIGHTEENTH AMENDMENT

The temperance movement promotes the moderation of or complete abstinence from the consumption of alcoholic beverages. It typically criticizes intoxication, promotes alcohol education and favors the passage of laws to regulate the availability and sale or the complete prohibition of alcoholic beverages.

The temperance movement evolved into a mass national movement in the late 1800s. It became very politically oriented and was influential in passing local, state and municipal legislation in many parts of the nation that affected alcohol consumption and sales. Other laws included the hours alcohol could be sold, the types of alcoholic beverages that businesses could stock, licensing of alcohol sales and the types of education that would be taught in schools that related to the effects of alcohol on the body, family and society.

In 1789, the first temperance society in the United States was founded by prominent citizens and businessmen in Litchfield County, Connecticut. They believed that the abuse of alcohol was negatively affecting people's ability to run businesses and was a hindrance to their local community and economy.

Other temperance societies were established throughout the nation during the eighteenth, nineteenth and early twentieth centuries. Temperance supporters were known as the "drys," and they adopted arguments and strategies and used various forms of propaganda and misinformation in an attempt to close the nation's breweries, distilleries and saloons. The drys

Dr. Benjamin Rush painted by Charles Willson Peale, circa 1783. *Courtesy of Wikimedia Commons.*

were predominantly White Protestants living in rural and small-town areas.

The opponents of temperance societies, and proponents of alcohol use, were known as the "wets," and they considered any bans on alcohol a violation of personal and societal freedoms. The wets were predominately urban residents of diverse religious and ethnic backgrounds. Many wets were newer immigrants to the United States. (Nearly twelve million immigrants arrived in the United States between 1870 and 1900.)

Dr. Benjamin Rush (1745–1813) was an educator, physician and signer of the Declaration of Independence. In 1790, he published *An Inquiry into the Effects of Spirituous Liquors on the Human Body.* This pamphlet highlighted several problems associated with drinking alcoholic beverages. Dr. Rush created a diagram called "A Moral and Physical Thermometer," which was intended to discourage the excessive use of alcohol by graphically displaying the dangers of intemperance. Rush's descriptions of the moral depravity and societal problems associated with excessive alcohol consumption helped fuel the early temperance movement for many years.

Many early temperance movement advocates believed that drunkards were in danger of spontaneous combustion because of their high blood pressure levels. This claim has been refuted by modern medicine.

Two of the pioneering temperance societies before the American Civil War (1861–65) were the American Temperance Society (ATS) and the American Temperance Union (ATU).

On February 13, 1826, the American Society for the Promotion of Temperance was founded. Later, it became known as the ATS. By 1831, it had grown to 2,200 chapters around the nation and included 170,000 members who had pledged to abstain from drinking distilled beverages (not including beer and wine). By 1836, the ATS had over 8,000 chapters and more than 1,250,000 members who had taken the pledge. The ATS did approve of the medicinal use of liquor.

In 1836, the ATU was founded with a goal to promote temperance. The ATU's publications of books, pamphlets, reports and especially its *Journal of the American Temperance Union* for adults and the *Youth's Temperance Advocate* for juveniles were very effective in promoting the temperance movement.

In 1851, the temperance movement influenced Maine to become the first state to prohibit the consumption and sale of alcohol. Maine's dry law set a precedent around the nation.

In 1861, when the American Civil War started, the temperance movement came to a halt as the nation's attention was obviously concentrated on the war. The American Civil War brought about additional problems, as many soldiers abused alcohol and some were even inebriated while on duty.

After the war ended, the temperance movement was resurrected and began reorganizing. Its activists became determined to turn the public against alcohol consumption and to convince the government to legally prohibit alcoholic beverages.

In 1873, a women's crusade against alcohol started in Ohio and included civil disobedience through public marches and the pressuring of alcohol-serving establishments. This movement spread throughout the country, and they were successful in closing over one thousand alcohol-serving establishments. By 1876, the women's crusade had begun to lose momentum, and many of the shuttered alcohol-serving establishments began to open along with new competitors.

One of the most notorious of all temperance movement crusaders was Caroline "Carrie" Amelia Nation (1846–1911). She was an extremist of the temperance movement and was also referred to as "Hatchet Granny." Nation claimed that divine intervention prompted her to destroy alcohol-serving establishments and described herself as "a bulldog running along at the feet of Jesus, barking at what He doesn't like."

She was mostly known for attacks in alcohol-serving saloons and taverns, where she smashed property with a hatchet. Between 1900 and 1910, she was arrested more than thirty times for what she called "Hatchetations" in various cities, including Kansas City, Wichita and Washington, D.C. Many of her fines were paid from lecture-tour income and from the sale of souvenir stickpins and miniature hatchets.

Her fame spread across the nation, and many alcohol-serving establishments hung signs with the slogan, "All Nations Are Welcome Except Carrie."

As her fame dissipated, she began appearing in vaudeville acts in the United States and music halls in England. She died on June 9, 1911, nine years shy of seeing her dream of nationwide Prohibition come true.

The Prohibition Party became an important part of the temperance movement with its historic political opposition to the sale or consumption of

Portrait of Carrie Nation, circa 1895. *Courtesy of Wikimedia Commons.*

alcoholic beverages. The Woman's Christian Temperance Union (WCTU) and then the Anti-Saloon League (ASL) became powerful temperance societies.

The Prohibition Party was founded on September 1, 1869. During the late nineteenth and early twentieth centuries, it evolved into an important third political party supporting women's suffrage, equal pay, income tax and other progressive ideology. Two Prohibition Party candidates who were elected into high-level offices were Sidney Catts (governor of Florida, served one term from 1917 to 1921) and Charles Randall (U.S. House of Representatives from California's Ninth District, served three terms from 1915 to 1921).

The WCTU was founded on December 23, 1873, in Hillsboro, Ohio. It became one of the largest and most influential women's groups of the nineteenth century as it advocated for the right to vote for women, prison reform, labor laws and Prohibition.

Frances Willard was a teacher, suffragist and co-founder of the WCTU. She was mostly homeschooled by her mother and briefly did attend a one-room school. In 1859, she graduated from the North Western Female College. Soon after, she began a career as a teacher. In 1871, she was hired as president of the Evanston College for Ladies. In 1873, the college merged with Northwestern University, and she became the dean of women of the women's college.

In 1874, she resigned and began a career in the women's temperance movement and became a co-founder of the WCTU. In 1879, Willard was elected president of the WCTU. She guided the WCTU to become the largest women's organization in the nineteenth century.

Since women could not vote in the United States until 1920, Willard urged women to lobby, petition, educate, make public appearances and write letters to local, state and national politicians in support of social changes. Willard became one of the most famous women in the world and grew the WCTU to 150,000 members.

Her health deteriorated rapidly, and she died in the Empire Hotel in New York City on February 17, 1898. Her influence lived on into the twentieth century and was instrumental in the passing of the Eighteenth Amendment and the Nineteenth Amendment (women's suffrage).

The Anti-Saloon League was founded in 1893 in Oberlin, Ohio, and was driven by evangelical Protestantism. It rapidly became the most powerful Prohibition lobby group in the nation and eventually overshadowed the WCTU.

Left: Portrait of Frances Willard, circa 1890. *Right*: Portrait of Wayne Wheeler, circa 1915. *Courtesy of Wikimedia Commons.*

Wayne B. Wheeler (1869–1927) was a longtime leader of the Anti-Saloon League and one of the most powerful temperance movement crusaders in the United States. In 1894, after graduating from Oberlin College, he accepted a position as an organizer for the ASL. In 1898, he earned his LLB degree from Western Reserve University while working for the ASL.

One of Wheeler's defining moments was when he led a campaign to unseat Ohio governor Myron T. Herrick in 1905. Wheeler gained national recognition as this prominent anti-Prohibition governor was ousted from office.

In 1915, Wheeler relocated to Washington, D.C., and began pressuring politicians to support Prohibition regardless of their party affiliation. This tactic of pressure politics has become known as Wheelerism. Wheeler guided the ASL to become the most powerful lobbyist group in U.S. history. He eventually controlled the balance of power in both the Democratic and Republican Parties without official authority.

There is no doubt that Wheeler and the ASL played an instrumental, if not leading, role in the passage of the Eighteenth Amendment.

The Wet Movement Struggles for Its Survival

The wet movement (anti-Prohibitionists who supported the use and legality of alcohol) used tactics such as bribery of government and elected officials, sponsoring newspaper advertisements that favored alcohol and paying poll taxes so poor immigrants could afford to vote in an effort to keep states from voting themselves dry.

In 1862, representatives of the nation's thirty-seven breweries (all German immigrants) founded the Lager-Beer Brewers Association, later named the United States Brewers' Association (USBA) in 1864. It started out as a trade organization concerned with taxation issues during the American Civil War. In 1867, the USBA began its challenge of the temperance movement and the emerging Prohibition Party.

One of the major leaders of the wet movement was Adolphus Busch (1839–1913), owner of the largest brewery in the Western Hemisphere. Busch began marketing beer as the family-friendly alternative to the higher alcohol content of liquor, which was attributed as being served in unruly saloons. This strategy caused conflict between breweries and distilleries and actually weakened the wet movement.

In 1898, Congress raised the tax on beer by one dollar a barrel to support the costs of the Spanish-American War (April 21, 1898–December 10, 1898).

Between 1900 and 1913, alcohol consumption significantly rose. This was mainly due to beer production, which increased from 1.2 billion to 2 billion gallons. During this period, the wet movement shortsightedly began to believe that anti-Prohibition momentum was swinging its way. However, the temperance movement continually put pressure on politicians and maintained a very loud and visible public profile, which led to growing anti-alcohol sentiments.

In 1901, the sale of alcohol was banned on all U.S. Army bases, which weakened the national influence of the wet movement.

In 1902, strong lobbying by the USBA led to the abolishment of the beer barrel tax increase.

In 1913, the Sixteenth Amendment (national income tax) was passed, which reduced the national government's reliance on tax revenues from alcohol sales. Prior to the Sixteenth Amendment, there were some years when 70 percent of the federal government's revenue came from alcohol excise taxes.

During World War I (1914–18; the United States entered in 1917), national income tax actually replaced liquor taxes as the primary source of federal revenue. The federal government also sanctioned the sales of grains to breweries and distilleries during the war.

World War I fueled anti-German and anti–German American propaganda that weakened the power of breweries and distilleries (most owned by German Americans). This propaganda linked beer and liquor with treason, as Germany was now an enemy of the United States. Prior to World War I, more than one thousand breweries existed, but within a few months after the United States entered the war, the number had shrunk to fewer than five hundred.

World War I was a major catalyst that severely weakened the wet movement. The ASL used the weakening of the USBA's lobbying influence, propaganda and new federal government laws and regulations to its advantage as it gained more support for the temperance movement all around the nation.

A temperance parade with women and children on a horse-drawn wagon. Two signs read: "We Can't Vote—Neither Can 'Ma'—If Florida Stays Wet Blame It onto 'Pa.'" Eustis, Florida, circa 1910. *Courtesy of State Archives of Florida.*

FLORIDA GOES DRY BEFORE NATIONWIDE PROHIBITION

Florida, like most states, was divided between the wets and the drys. Debates and arguments over regulating and banning alcohol in Florida started long before the Eighteenth Amendment.

In 1885, Florida adopted a new state constitution that included the option for each county to decide, by citizen voting, to ban or allow alcohol sales. By 1905, over half of the counties in Florida had voted to go dry.

In 1908, Carry Nation of "hatchet fame" toured Florida making speeches in support of a statewide prohibition law and attracted crowds in some cities of over two thousand. She told the crowd in Bradenton that she had been in jail thirty-two times in as many places, and her enemies had even tried to have her adjudged insane. All of this she considered her work on behalf of the prohibition of alcoholic beverages. Nation drew the largest crowd at the big tent in the history of Miami. Her presence in Florida surely gathered more supporters for the dry cause within the state.

In 1910, a statewide prohibition amendment did not win approval, but prohibition supporters continued their vigorous efforts to gain the majority of votes.

By 1913, Maine, West Virginia, North Carolina, Georgia, Tennessee, Mississippi, Oklahoma, Kansas and North Dakota all passed laws banning alcohol statewide. Florida was following the lead of these states as prohibitionists were making steady progress toward a statewide ban on alcohol. Even Miami-Dade County voted itself dry in 1913. By 1915, only twelve counties in Florida were wet, and statewide prohibition appeared to be inevitable.

Portrait of Florida's twenty-second governor, Sidney Johnston Catts, circa 1917. *Courtesy of State Archives of Florida.*

In 1916, the Democratic Party had several candidates running for governor, including William V. Knott, the state's comptroller, and Sidney J. Catts, a Baptist minister who campaigned throughout the state denouncing Catholicism and promoting statewide prohibition.

In June 1916, the Democratic primary votes pointed to an upset victory by Sidney J. Catts. However, Knott demanded a recount of the votes, and the Florida Supreme Court agreed. The recount gave Knott the victory by only twenty-

WHO WAS ANDREW VOLSTEAD?

Andrew Volstead was born on October 31, 1859, in Kenyon, Minnesota. He is mostly remembered for sponsoring the Volstead Act (the National Prohibition Act of 1919) as chair of the House Judiciary Committee. It is known that Wayne Wheeler of the Anti-Saloon League was instrumental in drafting the bill, but Volstead took most of the credit. Volstead was not a teetotaler, as he did occasionally drink alcoholic beverages.

In 1903, Volstead was elected to the U.S. House of Representatives as a member of the Republican Party and served until 1923. He supported civil rights and was one of the few congressmen to advocate federal legislation against lynching.

Volstead refused to talk about the Volstead Act or how it was being enforced; however, he was instrumental in defeating every congressional bill that was focused on modifying it. He received death threats and boxes of hate mail and was often referred to as the "Father of Prohibition."

An article in the *Baltimore Sun* asked Volstead: "How does it feel to be 'cussed' from coast to coast, as a rabid and fanatical 'dry,' when really you are a 'half wet' and it was merely the fortunes of politics that caused your name to go on a prohibition law?" Volstead referred to this as a "fake story."

Volstead was a staunch supporter of farmers, and in 1922, he co-sponsored the Capper-Volstead Act, which permitted farmers to form associations legally under the Sherman Antitrust Act.

Volstead was defeated in his congressional reelection campaign in 1922. In 1924, he was hired by the chief of the Prohibition Bureau as a legal advisor and served in that role until Prohibition was repealed in 1933.

On March 29, 1926, Volstead was featured on the cover of *Newsweek*.

After Prohibition, Volstead returned to practice law in Granite Falls, Minnesota. He died on January 20, 1947, in Granite Falls, Minnesota.

one votes. Catts and many of his supporters claimed they were cheated by the recount. Catts then entered the governor's race as a candidate of the Prohibition Party.

On Election Day in November 1916, Sidney Catts won the Florida governor's office by a margin of 9,200 votes. He became the only non-Democrat to become governor of Florida since the end of Reconstruction in 1877. With the Prohibition Party in the governor's seat and the growing number of dry counties, Florida was well on course to become a dry state.

In 1918, another attempt to ratify a statewide prohibition amendment was presented to Florida voters. Florida Prohibition, Amendment 2 passed by 61.62 percent of the vote. Statewide prohibition in Florida went into effect on January 1, 1919.

Florida Prohibition, Amendment 2 made the manufacture, sale, barter or exchange of all alcoholic or intoxicating liquors and beverages, whether spirituous, vinous or malt, illegal. The exceptions were alcohol for medical, scientific or mechanical purposes and wine for sacramental purposes, which were regulated by law. A heavy penalty for intoxication to the tune of a $500 fine was also mandated.

On November 27, 1918, Florida also ratified the Eighteenth Amendment to the U.S. Constitution.

On January 16, 1919, Nebraska became the thirty-sixth state to ratify the Eighteenth Amendment, which banned the manufacture, sale and transportation of alcohol across the entire nation.

On October 28, 1919, the National Prohibition Act, informally known as the Volstead Act, was passed by Congress and provided the law enforcement for the Eighteenth Amendment. Andrew Volstead, member of the U.S. House of Representatives from Minnesota, was the key promoter and facilitator of the bill.

Nationwide Prohibition, the once improbable goal of the drys, would go into effect the following year.

Chapter 3

NATIONWIDE PROHIBITION

The United States Goes "Bone Dry"

On January 16, 1920, the entire nation went dry as the Eighteenth Amendment to the U.S. Constitution prohibited the manufacture, sale or transportation of intoxicating liquors.

Most parts of the Constitution guarantee civil rights, liberties and individual freedoms, but nationwide Prohibition actually stripped some individual rights and limited specific freedoms.

The manufacture and distribution of alcoholic beverages was once the fifth-largest industry in the United States, but Prohibition made it illegal (with the exception of uses for medicinal, industrial and religious services). Thousands of alcohol beverage industry workers (mostly newer immigrants) lost their jobs. Hundreds of thousands of workers in related industries and occupations, such as barrel makers, bartenders, beverage distributors, bottlers, truck drivers and waitresses, lost their jobs as well. Prohibition caused an unemployment problem in many areas around the nation.

Initially, millions of people stopped drinking alcoholic beverages due to Prohibition laws. However, the legions who continued to drink alcoholic beverages, including more and more women, drank larger quantities. These increasing abuses of alcoholic beverages also led to additional cases of cirrhosis of the liver.

Prohibition laws forced licensed bars, nightclubs and saloons to close down. However, most were quickly replaced by unregulated speakeasies (illicit liquor shops and drinking clubs), which supplied alcoholic beverages (some smuggled into the country and others made by moonshiners and home brewers) to anyone who could pay their prices.

Eighteenth Amendment

Section 1.

After one year from the ratification of this article the manufacture, sale, or transportation of intoxicating liquors within, the importation thereof into, or the exportation thereof from the United States and all territory subject to the jurisdiction thereof for beverage purposes is hereby prohibited.

Section 2.

The Congress and the several States shall have concurrent power to enforce this article by appropriate legislation.

Section 3.

This article shall be inoperative unless it shall have been ratified as an amendment to the Constitution by the legislatures of the several States, as provided in the Constitution, within seven years from the date of the submission hereof to the States by the Congress.

At the beginning of Prohibition, the federal responsibility for enforcing the Volstead Act was split between the Treasury and Justice Departments. The Treasury Department created the Prohibition Unit (a section of the Bureau of Internal Revenue), which was tasked with gathering evidence and arresting lawbreakers. The Justice Department was tasked with the prosecution of lawbreakers. The United States Marshals Service (USMS), within the Department of Justice, operated under the direction of the U.S. attorney general and provided the principal federal enforcing agents. The Bureau of Investigation (BOI) acted in an emergency role for enforcement of Prohibition laws due to understaffing in the USMS.

In 1927, the U.S. Congress transferred the enforcement of Prohibition to the Department of Justice and created the Bureau of Prohibition (formerly the Prohibition Unit of the Bureau of Internal Revenue).

NATION BONE DRY AFTER MIDNIGHT

Nationwide Prohibition Becomes Effective at 12:01 Tonight—Wine, Beer or Liquor Can Neither Be Manufactured, Transported or Sold

ANCIENT DREAM OF THE "DRY" IS A FACT NOW

CONSTITUTIONAL PROHIBITION IS IN EFFECT

BILLY SUNDAY PRESIDES

Preaches Funeral Oration Over "Corpse" of "J. Barleycorn" While "Devil" Mourns

Top, left: "Nation Bone Dry After Midnight." *From the* Palm Beach Post, *January 16, 1920.*

Top, right: "Ancient Dream of the 'Dry' Is a Fact Now." *From the* Tampa Tribune, *January 17, 1920.*

Bottom: A masked criminal at the grave of John Barleycorn (a symbol or slang term for alcohol). *Judge*, October 29, 1921. *Courtesy of Wikimedia Commons.*

THE NATIONAL PROHIBITION CASES: U.S. SUPREME COURT DECISION

In 1920, seven legal cases, called the National Prohibition Cases, challenged the constitutionality of national Prohibition under the Eighteenth Amendment and certain general features of the National Prohibition Act, commonly called the Volstead Act.

The lead case was *State of Rhode Island v. A. Mitchell Palmer, Attorney General, and Daniel C. Roper, Commissioner of Internal Revenue* (six other cases were grouped together and heard, and a collective decision was rendered). The main argument by the plaintiffs was based on what they considered to be procedural defects.

On June 7, 1920, Justice Willis Van Devanter announced that the Supreme Court, by a decision of seven to two, upheld the Eighteenth Amendment and the Volstead Act.

MABEL WALKER WILLEBRANDT: "DRY CZARINA"

During the 1920s, Mabel Walker Willebrandt was known by most people in the nation as she became the public face of Prohibition enforcement and the most famous non–movie star woman in America. Her relentless pursuit of enforcing the legalities of the Volstead Act made her well known to most moonshiners, bootleggers, rumrunners and most certainly all organized crime syndicates and their bosses. Her notoriety gained her many nicknames in the press, including "Dry Czarina," "Little Miss Trouble," "Prohibition Portia" and the "First Lady of Law."

Mabel Walker was born on May 23, 1889, in Woodsdale, Kansas. She was an only child. Her parents moved frequently while pursuing various teaching and printing jobs. She was homeschooled until age thirteen. She then attended public school and graduated from high school.

After high school, she became a teacher and in 1910 married Arthur Willebrandt, the school's principal. Due to Arthur's suffering from tuberculosis, the couple moved to the dry climate of Arizona. She obtained a job as a teacher, supported Arthur while he recuperated and attended and graduated from the Tempe Normal School, now Arizona State University, in 1911.

Mabel Walker Willebrandt, the First Lady of Law, circa 1925. *Courtesy of Wikimedia Commons.*

In 1916, the Willebrandts separated, and their divorce was finalized in 1924.

She became the City of Los Angeles's first female public defender and mostly handled cases involving prostitutes. During World War I, Willebrandt was head of Los Angeles's Legal Advisory Board, where she dealt with military draft cases.

In 1921, she was recommended by several people—including law professor Frank Doherty and Senator Hiram Johnson—for the post of assistant U.S. attorney general. President Warren G. Harding decided to appoint her to that post. In 1921, at thirty-two years old, she became the highest-ranking woman in the federal government and only the second woman in U.S. history to hold the position of assistant U.S. attorney general.

Willebrandt was assigned head of the federal taxation division of the Justice Department, Bureau of Federal Prisons, and handled cases concerning violations of the Volstead Act. She was burdened with one of the heaviest responsibilities of any appointed official in the federal government during the Prohibition era.

Willebrandt became a strong enforcer of the Volstead Act and also a teetotaler. She fired hundreds of corrupt and incompetent federal employees and replaced them with educated and better-trained people in an all-out effort to enforce Prohibition.

She realized that in order to stop the numerous small bootleggers, the large operations at the top of the smuggling rings had to be shuttered. Her efforts to expand the U.S. Coast Guard led to a significant decline of rumrunning off the coast of Florida and other parts of the Atlantic coast. She was also credited with busting two of the largest bootlegging operations in the nation (located in Mobile, Alabama, and Savannah, Georgia) and apprehending their leaders.

In 1927, Willebrandt successfully argued in front of the U.S. Supreme Court that taxes should be paid on illegal income. This decision allowed the Internal Revenue Service to build income tax evasion cases against mobsters, including Al Capone.

Since the number of women being arrested during Prohibition doubled, Willebrandt petitioned Congress for the funds to build a new federal prison for women. The nation's first federal prison for women opened in Alderson, West Virginia, in 1929.

In 1928, Willebrandt rigorously campaigned for the Republican presidential candidate, Herbert Hoover. After Hoover won the presidency, it is speculated that he was hesitant to promote her to U.S. attorney general because Prohibition was becoming very unpopular, and she was the public face of its enforcement. The Hoover administration also turned her down for a federal judgeship.

After being snubbed by the Hoover administration, Willebrandt resigned from her office in May 1929. She returned to Los Angeles and opened a private law practice specializing in radio and aeronautical law. She also represented many Hollywood celebrities, including Louis B. Mayer, Clark Gable, Jean Harlow and the MGM Studios. She was also involved with the drafting of the Screen Directors Guild's controversial loyalty oath against Communism during the Red Scare (1947–57).

Willebrandt died from lung cancer on April 6, 1963. She never received the proper credit she deserved for her incredible achievements as assistant U.S. attorney general.

"Give me the authority and let me have my pick of three hundred men and I'll make this country as dry as it is humanly possible. There's one way it can be done—get at the source of supply. I know them and I know how they could be cut off. I have no patience with this policy of going after the hip-pocket and speakeasy cases. That's like trying to dry up the Atlantic Ocean with a blotter."
—Mabel Walker Willebrandt

Loopholes in the Volstead Act

There were several loopholes in the Volstead Act that allowed alcoholic beverages to be legally obtained. One of the most interesting things about the Volstead Act was that the drinking of alcoholic beverages and the making of wine at home for personal consumption were legal. It was legal for people to make and consume up to 200 gallons of wine per year in their homes. This is equivalent to two and a half 750-milliliter bottles of wine per day, per household. During Prohibition, it was estimated that home winemaking increased to nine times its pre-Prohibition rate.

Private clubs were allowed to stockpile any amount of alcoholic beverages they purchased prior to Prohibition going into effect. Some exclusive private clubs stored enough alcoholic beverages to supply their members for many years after Prohibition began.

"Prohibition only drives drunkenness behind doors and into dark places, and does not cure it or even diminish it."
–Mark Twain

Licensed medical doctors could prescribe medicinal alcohol for conditions including cancer, depression, high blood pressure and indigestion. This led to many pharmacies becoming fronts for bootlegging operations.

Many industries were permitted to use various types of industrial alcohol for production operations. This led to the theft of large amounts of these supplies that were then used for human consumption.

Religious organizations were permitted to purchase alcoholic beverages for use in ceremonies and regular worship services. This led to an increase in alcohol orders for many religious congregations and an increase in parishioner enrollments. Also, many fake clergymen distributed alcohol to nonreligious congregations.

MEDICINAL LIQUOR: LEGAL DURING PROHIBITION

Prohibition required medical doctors to obtain a special permit from the federal government to write prescriptions for liquor. Patients could purchase liquor from a pharmacy with a prescription form for medicinal liquor that was completed and signed by a licensed medical doctor. Patients of all ages were prescribed alcohol, usually whiskey or brandy, for a wide variety of ailments. The common adult dose was usually about one ounce every two to three hours, and the common children's doses usually ranged from one-half to two teaspoons every three hours.

The Willis-Campell Act of 1921 (commonly known as the "Beer Emergency Bill") clarified Prohibition regulations for the medicinal use of alcohol. This law stated that only "spirituous and vinous liquors," which included spirits and wine, could be prescribed for medicinal use. The law excluded beer for medicinal use. It also reduced the amount of alcohol per prescription to a half pint and limited medical doctors to writing one hundred prescriptions over a ninety-day period for medicinal alcohol.

INSTRUCTIONS

Both this ORIGINAL and the DUPLICATE thereof must be delivered to the druggist.

This prescription form is INVALID AFTER 3 DAYS following date of issuance unless extended by prescribing physician not exceeding 3 days.

The physician issuing and the druggist filling this prescription must be satisfied of the respective bonafides in each case with reference to patient's identity, domicile, medical need and limitations as to time and quantity.

Misrepresentation of name, address or medical need for the purposes of fraudulently obtaining this prescription is unlawful.

Druggists are authorized to refuse to fill illegible or improperly executed prescriptions.

Failure to comply with the provisions of the law in the issuance and filling of this prescription will subject the permittee to citation for revocation of permit.

THIS ORIGINAL PRESCRIPTION MUST BE FORWARDED by the druggist to the office of the Prohibition Administrator before the TENTH day of the ensuing month.

This original prescription is INVALID if it bears changes or alterations of any kind.

VOID UNLESS PRESENTED WITH THE DUPLICATE.

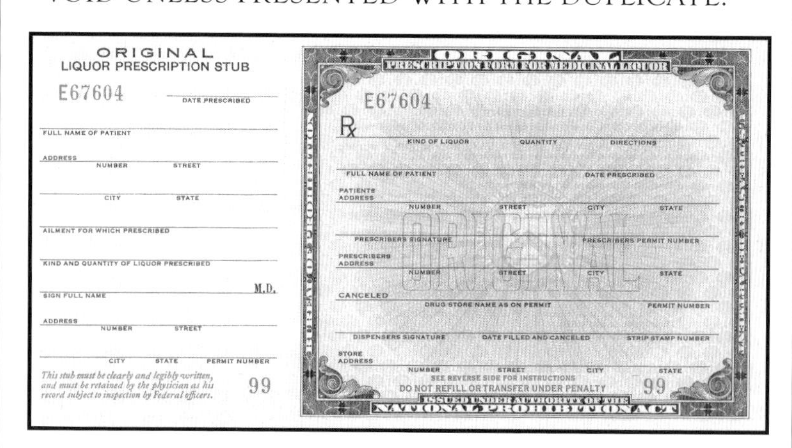

ORIGINAL
LIQUOR PRESCRIPTION STUB
E67604
DATE PRESCRIBED
FULL NAME OF PATIENT
ADDRESS NUMBER STREET
CITY STATE
AILMENT FOR WHICH PRESCRIBED
KIND AND QUANTITY OF LIQUOR PRESCRIBED
SIGN FULL NAME M.D.
ADDRESS NUMBER STREET
CITY STATE PERMIT NUMBER
This stub must be clearly and legibly written, and must be retained by the physician as his record subject to inspection by Federal officers.
99

ORIGINAL
PRESCRIPTION FORM FOR MEDICINAL LIQUOR
E67604
Rx
KIND OF LIQUOR QUANTITY DIRECTIONS
FULL NAME OF PATIENT DATE PRESCRIBED
PATIENTS ADDRESS NUMBER STREET CITY STATE
PRESCRIBERS SIGNATURE PRESCRIBERS PERMIT NUMBER
PRESCRIBERS ADDRESS NUMBER STREET CITY STATE
CANCELED
DRUG STORE NAME AS ON PERMIT PERMIT NUMBER
DISPENSERS SIGNATURE DATE FILLED AND CANCELED STRIP STAMP NUMBER
STORE ADDRESS NUMBER STREET CITY STATE
SEE REVERSE SIDE FOR INSTRUCTIONS
DO NOT REFILL OR TRANSFER UNDER PENALTY
99
ISSUED UNDER AUTHORITY OF THE
NATIONAL PROHIBITION ACT

Prescription Form for Medicinal Liquor (Number E67604)—ORIGINAL. *Author's collection and photograph.*

INSTRUCTIONS

Both this DUPLICATE prescription form and the ORIGINAL thereof must be delivered to the druggist.

This prescription form is INVALID AFTER 3 DAYS following date of issuance unless extended by prescribing physician not exceeding 3 days.

The physician issuing and the druggist filling this prescription must be satisfied of the respective bonafides in each case with reference to patient's identity, domicile, medical need and limitations as to time and quantity.

Misrepresentation of name, address or medical need for the purposes of fraudulently obtaining this prescription is unlawful.

Druggists are authorized to refuse to fill illegible or improperly executed prescriptions.

Failure to comply with the provisions of the law in the issuance and filling of this prescription will subject the permittee to citation for revocation of permit.

THIS DUPLICATE PRESCRIPTION MUST BE LEGIBLE and must be an exact copy of the accompanying original.

This duplicate prescription must be properly canceled by the druggist by filing in the information required by him on the face thereof.

THIS DUPLICATE PRESCRIPTION MUST BE RETAINED by the druggist as a permanent record, open to inspection by Federal Officers.

This duplicate prescription is INVALID if it bears changes or alterations of any kind.

VOID UNLESS PRESENTED WITH THE ORIGINAL.

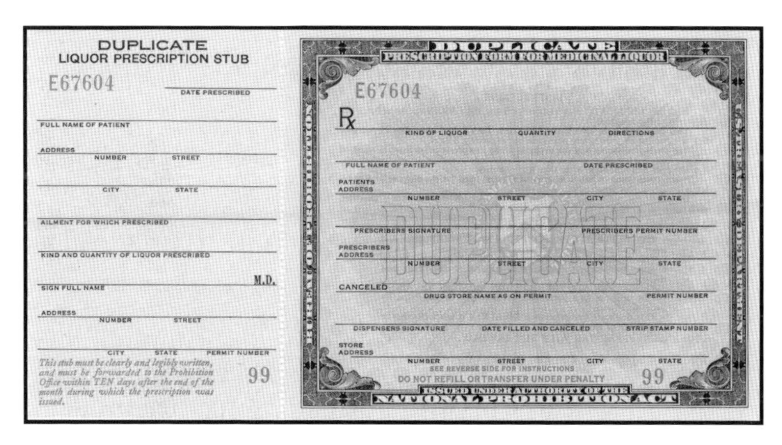

DUPLICATE
LIQUOR PRESCRIPTION STUB
E67604
DATE PRESCRIBED
FULL NAME OF PATIENT
ADDRESS NUMBER STREET
CITY STATE
AILMENT FOR WHICH PRESCRIBED
KIND AND QUANTITY OF LIQUOR PRESCRIBED
M.D.
SIGN FULL NAME
ADDRESS NUMBER STREET
CITY STATE PERMIT NUMBER
This stub must be clearly and legibly written, and must be forwarded to the Prohibition Office within TEN days after the end of the month during which the prescription was issued.
99

DUPLICATE
PRESCRIPTION FORM FOR MEDICINAL LIQUOR
E67604
℞
KIND OF LIQUOR QUANTITY DIRECTIONS
FULL NAME OF PATIENT DATE PRESCRIBED
PATIENTS ADDRESS NUMBER STREET CITY STATE
PRESCRIBERS SIGNATURE PRESCRIBERS PERMIT NUMBER
PRESCRIBERS ADDRESS NUMBER STREET CITY STATE
DUPLICATE
CANCELED
DRUG STORE NAME AS ON PERMIT PERMIT NUMBER
DISPENSERS SIGNATURE DATE FILLED AND CANCELED STRIP STAMP NUMBER
STORE ADDRESS NUMBER STREET CITY STATE
SEE REVERSE SIDE FOR INSTRUCTIONS
DO NOT REFILL OR TRANSFER UNDER PENALTY
99
ISSUED UNDER AUTHORITY OF THE
NATIONAL PROHIBITION ACT

Prescription Form for Medicinal Liquor (Number E67604)—DUPLICATE. *Author's collection and photograph.*

Many medical doctors at the time considered Prohibition, and the Willis-Campbell Act, an encroachment on their profession, as these limitations were considered to be unwarranted government oversight.

It is estimated that medical doctors wrote 11 million medicinal alcohol prescriptions per year throughout the 1920s. This was a period when the population in the United States ranged from 106 to 123 million, so that is a significant number of medicinal alcohol prescriptions.

The Bible has some interesting references about alcoholic beverages, including: "Go, eat your bread with joy, and drink your wine with a merry heart, for God has already approved what you do."
–Ecclesiastes 9:7

Jamaica Ginger ("Jake")

Jamaica ginger extract was a medicine used as a remedy for various conditions, including headaches, intestinal gas, menstrual disorders and upper respiratory infections. It contained 70 to 80 percent ethanol alcohol. During Prohibition, people drank it because of its high alcohol content.

At the beginning of Prohibition, Jamaica ginger was available without a prescription and could be purchased over the counter. In 1921, the federal government made the original formulation of Jamaica ginger a prescription-only product.

By 1931, an estimated 100,000 people had been afflicted with paralysis of the hands and feet. These conditions are referred to as Jamaica ginger paralysis or Jake paralysis. The tri-orthocresyl phosphate (TOCP) compound in Jamaica ginger is a slow-acting neurotoxin that causes numbness, weakness, foot drop and eventual paralysis. Recovery from the disease is very slow, and many afflicted people wound up with permanent neurological damage. Many of the victims were poor immigrants and received little medical care or governmental assistance.

The Ku Klux Klan: Staunch Supporters of Prohibition

The Ku Klux Klan (KKK) is a white supremacist, anti–African American, anti-Semitic, anti-Catholic, anti-immigrant, right-wing domestic terrorist and hate group founded in 1865 by six former army officers of the Confederate States of America.

The KKK's first grand wizard (national leader) was the infamous slave trader and Confederate cavalry general Nathan Bedford Forrest, who was the perpetrator of the Fort Pillow Massacre during the American Civil War. Forrest's men opened fire and slaughtered Black and White U.S. Army soldiers after they surrendered.

The KKK became an extreme militant wing of the temperance movement and was one of the major proponents of Prohibition. The group supported anti-alcohol initiatives and laws vigorously and sometimes violently. Support around the nation for the KKK surged during Prohibition.

Many white Protestants who supported Prohibition did not think law enforcement was doing enough to stop bootleggers and rumrunners. The KKK was able to convince many of these people that they were a vigilante police group who could stop Catholic immigrants and other anti-Prohibition supporters from violating Prohibition laws. The KKK was able to gain community support as it claimed it would clean up towns by eliminating bootleggers and moonshiners and close down speakeasies.

Ku Klux Klan march in downtown Brooksville, Florida, February 24, 1922. *Courtesy of State Archives of Florida.*

The KKK raided and terrorized the homes and businesses of immigrants, Blacks and other anti-Prohibition supporters. Structures were often burned, and people were beaten and occasionally lynched. When alcoholic beverages were seized, the cache was oftentimes destroyed and sometimes kept to hypocritically drink among themselves.

By 1925, the KKK had between two and five million members, including an auxiliary Women of the Ku Klux Klan and several youth groups. Many additional millions of people around the nation supported them and their activities.

The KKK forcibly opposed the illegal sale of alcohol and especially targeted bootleggers. They burned speakeasies, hijacked and destroyed illegal shipments of alcohol, tarred and feathered suspected bootleggers and ran them out of town and flogged and killed an unknown number of people.

An example of the KKK's Prohibition-era violence in Florida is the December 1921 attack on Manuel Cabeza, a decorated World War I veteran and owner of the Red Rooster coffee shop (one of many illicit speakeasies that operated in Key West at the time). Cabeza was targeted by the KKK for both operating a speakeasy and for moving his mistress, a "mulatto" prostitute, into housing behind his business. A mob of five carloads of Klansmen dragged Cabeza from his home and beat, tarred and feathered and ordered him to leave town or die. A few days later, Cabeza hunted down one of his attackers, Exalted Cyclops Walter Decker, and shot and killed him. After surviving the wrath of a Klan posse, Cabeza was arrested and jailed. A group of U.S. Marines guarded the jailhouse, but Monroe County sheriff Roland Curry dismissed them. Soon after, a lynch mob consisting of fifteen Klansmen broke into the jailhouse and kidnapped Cabeza. The Klansmen dragged him through the streets of Key West while tied to a car, beat, hanged and riddled his dead body with a barrage of bullets. No one was ever prosecuted for Cabeza's gruesome murder.

Initial Reactions to Prohibition in Florida

When Prohibition began, many people followed the law, and the consumption of alcohol fell in Florida and around the nation.

On January 29, 1920, the *Tampa Bay Times* reported that H.L. Ermatinger, the former local leader of the wets who believed Prohibition would have ill effects on the Tampa Bay area, changed his allegiances to the dry forces. Ermatinger became the city and county chairman of the

Red's Place was a shack built on the beach in Daytona Beach by pilot and bootlegger Winder "Red" Cowan. It was a refueling station for aircraft and a front for the sales of illicit liquor that was flown in from the Caribbean. In 1932, a storm floated Red's Place into the ocean. *Courtesy of State Archives of Florida.*

Prohibition enforcement campaign and said, "I was of the opinion that Prohibition was not a good thing for this community and that it would hurt business here…I have now found that I was wrong; that Prohibition helped business here rather than hurt it, and I am not a bit ashamed to acknowledge that I was wrong."

H.L. Ermatinger's reaction to Prohibition was not shared by everyone in Florida, but it was representative of many local leaders who initially believed Prohibition could be enforced and was here to stay.

PROHIBITION AND FLORIDA'S SIGNIFICANT TOBACCO INDUSTRY

In 1920, the tobacco industry was a significant force in Florida. Ybor City was considered the "Cigar Capital of the World." Obviously, many jobs and a good portion of state revenue depended on the tobacco industry in Florida.

After the success of the drys getting the Eighteenth Amendment passed, talk of the evil parallels of tobacco to alcohol circulated around the nation,

A converted U.S. Navy patrol aircraft that carried passengers to the Bahama islands of Bimini and Nassau during Prohibition. *Courtesy of State Archives of Florida.*

especially by religious zealots, who suggested abolishing tobacco as well. Some people around Florida became concerned that tobacco could follow the fate of alcohol and have its use prohibited by national legislation.

In reality, most people in Florida and around the nation did not favor anti-tobacco legislation. The anti-tobacco movement never gained enough support to pass national legislation during Prohibition, and fears of tobacco's demise in Florida faded.

THE NEAREST "WET SPOT" TO FLORIDA

One way Floridians, and others, sidetracked Prohibition was to travel to other countries that allowed the consumption of alcohol. The Caribbean island of Bimini (the westernmost district of the Bahamas) was the nearest wet spot to Florida. The distance from Miami to Bimini is only fifty-six nautical miles.

During Prohibition, daily flights were scheduled in the winter season to Bimini and other areas of the Bahamas, where rum and other alcoholic beverages were served legally.

Chapter 4

PROHIBITION LAWS DEFIED BY THE MASSES AND THE ENTRUSTED

In the beginning, Prohibition seemed to be working, as alcohol consumption, public drunkenness and alcohol-related deaths all declined. However, many Americans believed Prohibition was absurd because the government was interfering in their lives. Its enforcement proved to be near impossible as the masses soon defied national anti-alcohol laws. Some trusted with the enforcement of Prohibition became corrupt as they discovered easy ways to make money and began exploiting the inherent inconsistencies in the law. This corruption contributed to a growing decline in public anti-alcohol support.

In 1925, Henry Lewis Mencken (the well-known journalist, essayist, satirist and social critic) wrote:

> *Five years of Prohibition have had, at least, this one benign effect: They have completely disposed of all the favorite arguments of the Prohibitionists. None of the great boons and usufructs that were to follow the passage of the 18th Amendment has come to pass. There is not less drunkenness in the Republic, but more. There is not less crime, but more. There is not less insanity, but more. The cost of government is not smaller, but vastly greater. Respect for law has not increased, but diminished.*

Scofflaw

In 1924, the *Boston Herald* offered a $200 prize for the creation of a new word that would describe a person who drinks illicit alcoholic beverages and blatantly ignores Prohibition laws. There were twenty-five thousand responses. Two readers split the prize as they came up with the same word: "scofflaw."

Originally, during the Prohibition era, the term *scofflaw* denoted flagrant defiance of anti-alcohol laws. Since then, it has been extended to denote people who openly disregard any law that is challenging to effectively enforce, including many traffic laws.

Speakeasies: Illicit Liquor Shops and Drinking Clubs

Speakeasies were very profitable illicit liquor shops and drinking clubs that became cultural icons during Prohibition. They were also called "blind pigs" and "gin joints." After Prohibition forced the closure of the traditional saloons and bars, illegal speakeasies opened almost everywhere around the nation. Speakeasies ranged from lavish nightclubs to small hole-in-the-wall bars. Some required membership cards or a "secret" password to enter.

Since speakeasies did not operate under governmental regulations, there were no age limits, set business hours or restrictions on serving any types of liquor, moonshine or bathtub gin (homemade poor-quality alcoholic beverages made from cheap grain alcohol, water and various flavoring agents).

Different from the now-defunct traditional male-only saloons, speakeasies were open to women. A liberation of women occurred as they were now drinking alcoholic beverages alongside men, staying out late and dancing the night away.

Flappers: Trendsetting Young Women of the 1920s

Flappers of the 1920s were young women known for their independent freedom who challenged societal barriers related to economic, political and sexual freedom. Their lifestyle was considered carefree, dangerous, immoral, outrageous, reckless and shocking to many at the time.

Life magazine cover, February 2, 1922: "The Flapper" by Frank Xavier Leyendecker. *Courtesy of Wikimedia Commons.*

Flappers were known for their trendsetting style, which included bobbed haircuts, above-the-knee dress lengths and the popularization of Jazz Age dancing such as the foxtrot, waltz and tango. They were also flaunting a disdain for what was then considered acceptable behavior for women by violating Prohibition laws and drinking illegal alcohol, driving automobiles, smoking cigarettes in public and wearing excessive makeup.

The women's suffrage movement finally earned women the right to vote via the Nineteenth Amendment to the Constitution in 1920. Women now had just as much say as men as to who got elected to political offices. With their newly found freedom and political power, flappers helped lead women away from the Victorian era's stranglehold, which dictated that a woman's proper role was to marry, have children, keep a clean house and be content within a household environment.

Lois Bancroft Long (1901–1974), famed journalist of the *New Yorker*, was the poster child of the flappers. She was born on December 15, 1901, in Stamford, Connecticut. In 1922, she graduated from the prestigious Vassar College (at the time it was strictly for women and considered a sister institution to the Ivy League). She started her journalism career at *Vogue* and *Vanity Fair*. In 1925, she was hired at the *New Yorker* by its founder, Harold Ross, to write a column about the flamboyant New York City nightlife. While

A staged joke photo of a young lady wearing stiffly formal and proper 1890s clothes (*at left*) pretending to be startled by a 1920s flapper (Lois Long, *at right*). *Courtesy of Wikimedia Commons.*

"Tomorrow we may die, so let's get drunk and make love."
–Lois Long

writing under the name of Lipstick, she chronicled her nightly escapades of drinking, dining and dancing at nightclubs and illegal speakeasies. She inadvertently invented fashion criticism (the form of rational critical writing that analyzes and evaluates various fashion styles, trends and designers).

Her intelligence, humor and literary style propelled her into celebrity status. She remained a mystery to legions of readers and often teased them by suggesting she was a "short squat maiden of forty" or a "kindly, old, bearded gentleman." The cat was let out of the bag in 1927 when her marriage to the *New Yorker* cartoonist Peter Arno was publicly announced. Now that her real identity was revealed, her readers loved her even more, as they realized she was living the actual exciting lifestyle of a flapper. Readers were enthralled with her reporting of the behind-the-scenes decadent stories of blatant Prohibition defiance. They were also thrilled to know that she was privy to the passwords that allowed her entry into the most notorious illegal speakeasies in New York City.

Long stayed with the *New Yorker* as a columnist and editor until 1968. She died in 1974 in Saratoga, New York.

The legacy of the flappers is linked to the changing of the lives of women throughout the United States as they forged newfound freedoms. Flappers also set the stage for the women's liberation movement that emerged in the late 1960s.

Prohibition Enables the Proliferation of Organized Crime

Before Prohibition, the term "organized crime" was not part of the vocabulary in the United States. Criminal gangs had existed since the late 1800s, but they were mostly street thugs running small extortion and loansharking operations in predominantly Irish, Italian, Jewish and Polish neighborhoods in cities around the United States. These criminal gangs were also oftentimes employed by corrupt local political bosses who controlled the underworld. The criminal gangs would intimidate opposing candidates and their supporters to ensure certain political bosses would receive the majority of the votes. As compensation, the corrupt political bosses would instruct the police to ignore the illegal activities of these criminal gangs.

Prohibition provided the opportunity for organized crime to emerge as criminal gangs capitalized on new racketeering operations related to illegal alcoholic beverages that were now available. Criminal gangs quickly organized bootlegging, rumrunning and speakeasy operations, which earned millions of dollars per year. This extraordinary amount of money allowed these criminals to hire lawyers and accountants to protect their illegal operations. They also bribed politicians, police and federal agents to turn a blind eye to their illegal operations. During Prohibition, control of the underworld shifted from corrupt political bosses to organized criminal syndicates and mobsters associated with organizations such as the Mafia.

"Making Prohibition work is like making water run uphill; it's against nature."
–Milton Friedman

AL CAPONE: FLORIDA'S INFAMOUS GANGSTER RESIDENT

The most infamous gangster in U.S. history was Alphonse Gabriele "Al" Capone. He was born in 1899 in Brooklyn, New York, to recent Italian immigrants. Prohibition provided the means for his rise to power and infamy. It is estimated that he earned $60 million per year selling illegal alcoholic beverages during Prohibition.

After dropping out of school, Capone started running errands for a local numbers and gambling operations criminal named Johnny Torrio. In 1909, Torrio relocated to Chicago, and Capone took a legitimate job as a paper cutter in a munitions factory but did participate in some criminal activity with street gangs in Brooklyn.

In 1917, Torrio introduced Capone to a gangster named Frankie Yale, who offered him a job as a bouncer and bartender at Coney Island's Harvard Inn. While working at the Harvard Inn, Capone obtained the nickname "Scarface" after making an indecent remark to a woman. As a result, her brother slashed Capone's face, causing the three very noticeable scars that marked him for life.

In 1919, Capone married Mae Coughlin, and they had a child named Albert Francis. He and his new family moved to Baltimore, where he took a legitimate job as a bookkeeper for a construction company.

In 1920, Capone's father died, and Torrio offered Capone a more lucrative opportunity as a mobster dealing in the gambling and prostitution rackets

Photograph of Al Capone wearing his favorite style fedora hat, circa 1928. *Courtesy of Wikimedia Commons.*

in Chicago. When Prohibition became the law of the land, Torrio diversified his rackets into the highly profitable bootlegging market. Capone's background as a street thug and bookkeeper quickly propelled him up the ladder in Torrio's syndicate, where he became a partner.

In 1923, Torrio and Capone moved their headquarters to the Chicago suburb of Cicero after a reformist mayor was elected who began investigating corruption. In 1924, Cicero's mayoral election threatened Torrio and Capone's illegal operations, so they threatened voters on election day, and several people were shot and killed. It was during this violence that Capone's brother Frank was gunned down in the street by local policemen.

In 1925, Torrio survived an assassination attempt, turned the entire illegal operation over to Capone and fled to Italy. Ignoring Torrio's advice to keep a low public profile, Capone moved his headquarters to the upscale Metropole Hotel in downtown Chicago. Capone began living a public and lavish lifestyle, spending huge sums of money (always in cash). The press followed Capone and treated him as a celebrity. Capone gained public compassion as anti-Prohibition resentment grew around the nation.

In 1926, Capone ordered a hit on two rival mobsters in Cicero. However, as his assassins gunned them down, they also mistakenly killed William McSwiggin, who was known as the "Hanging Prosecutor." Earlier, McSwiggin had attempted to prosecute Capone for murder. The public began to turn against Capone and organized crime in general because of the frequent public murders and lawlessness during the Prohibition era. Capone's house was raided, but no evidence linking him to these three murders was discovered.

Capone called a "Peace Conference" for Chicago's organized crime leaders, and it initially resulted in an agreement to stop the violence. However, peace did not last long, as Prohibition-related greed bred even more violence.

"Prohibition has made nothing but trouble."
–Al Capone

By the beginning of 1927, many efforts from rival gangsters, law enforcement and politicians were working to drive Capone out of Chicago. Feeling the heat from many angles, Capone announced he was going to St. Petersburg, Florida. Instead, he traveled to Los Angeles but was harassed by police and discovered he was not welcome in California. Capone decided to take a train back to Chicago, and at the stops along the way, he was badgered by local police.

In December 1927, Capone realized that he was wearing out his welcome in Chicago and that most other places did not want him, so he decided to go to Miami, Florida. Capone regarded Miami as "the garden of America, the sunny Italy of the New World, where life is good and abundant, where happiness is to be had even by the poorest." In the 1920s, Miami was also known for its unhindered gambling and lax enforcement of Prohibition. This seemed to Capone as the best place in the United States to hang loose for a while.

Capone booked the penthouse suite at the Ponce de Leon Hotel in downtown Miami. As soon as the community learned of Capone's presence, several local groups—including the Miami Beach Chamber of Commerce, the Women's Club and the Committee of One Hundred—lobbied Miami Beach Mayor J. Newton Lummus Jr. to oust him from the area. After Capone assured community leaders that he was in Miami to relax, they did nothing to force him to leave. Capone was good for business but was also an obvious public safety hazard.

The entrance of Al Capone's mansion in Palm Island, Florida, was located at 93 Palm Avenue. Capone bought the estate in 1928 as a winter retreat and lived there for several years. He died here in 1947. *Courtesy of Wikimedia Commons.*

Al Capone's Historic Miami Beach Home Demolished on August 11, 2023

Local preservationists could not save gangster Al Capone's one-time home on Miami Beach's Palm Island, and it has met the wrecking ball. Daniel Ciraldo, the executive director of the Miami Design Preservation League, said, "The growth of South Florida is very closely tied to the Prohibition era."

Capone became interested in a fourteen-room, two-story, white stucco Spanish architectural–style mansion at 93 Palm Island, Miami Beach. In March 1928, Capone purchased the property in his wife's name and began plans to settle in the Miami area.

Some of Capone's favorite pastimes were hosting elaborate dinner parties, marathon card games and betting on horse races at the Miami Jockey Club in Hialeah.

Capone was not content with participating in local gambling and allowing illegal speakeasies to operate without getting a cut of the action. He invested in several local establishments, including the Palm Island Club (gambling and speakeasy), the Floridian Hotel's gambling room, the South Beach dog track and the Villa Venice (casino).

On February 14, 1929, Capone and his top hit man, "Machine Gun" Jack McGurn, decided to kill longtime rival "Bugs" Moran. McGurn's assassins posed as policemen and brutally gunned down seven of Moran's men in a Chicago garage. Ironically, Bugs Moran was not present and escaped the hit, which is now known as the St. Valentine's Day Massacre.

At the time of the St. Valentine's Day Massacre, Capone was staying at his house on Palm Island in Miami, which provided his alibi to escape prosecution. Although he did not pull the trigger himself, he was blamed by the public and the media and was now considered Public Enemy Number One. Capone had earlier said, "Don't mistake my kindness for weakness. I am kind to everyone, but when someone is unkind to me, weak is not what you are going to remember about me." These words echoed through public sentiment as Capone's brutal violence turned his previous popularity to utter disdain.

The St. Valentine's Day Massacre created unwanted public, political and law enforcement attention on Prohibition-related illegal operations run by organized crime. Most of the prominent Midwest and East Coast crime families attended a conference at the President Hotel in Atlantic City from May 13 to 19, 1929. Capone convinced the crime bosses to spread the wealth, stop the killings and look forward to more cooperation among the families.

While waiting in Philadelphia to board a train to Chicago, Capone and fellow gangster Frank Rio were arrested at the Stanley Theater for carrying concealed weapons. Capone and Rio pleaded guilty and were surprised to receive a one-year prison sentence (the maximum allowed by law).

In March 1930, Capone was released from prison in Pennsylvania and decided to head back to Florida, as authorities in Chicago threatened to arrest him if he returned to the Windy City.

After Capone was freed from jail, public fascination with the Prohibition-era gangster peaked, as he was featured on the cover of the March 24, 1930 edition of *Time* magazine.

Capone's troubles with local law enforcement harassment in Florida escalated. Miami's director of public safety, Sam McCreary, ordered the police chief, Guy C. Reeve, to arrest Capone "anytime, anywhere, in any company, every time that he would set foot in the jurisdiction of the city of Miami." On May 8, 1930, he was arrested while heading to the Olympia Theater in Miami. On May 13, 1930, he and three associates were arrested while attending a boxing match at the American Legion Hall.

Mug shot of Al Capone taken at the Miami, Florida Police Department in May 1930. *Courtesy of State Archives of Florida.*

"I would rather be rich, affluent, and greedy and go to hell when I die, than live in poverty on this earth."
–Al Capone

On May 23, 1930, Miami City Commissioners passed a vagrancy ordinance directly targeting Capone. The ordinance was aimed at "anyone having visible means of support acquired in unlawful or illegal manner or persons dangerous to public safety or peace, and persons known to be crooks, gangsters or hijackers to be vagrants."

The inhospitable treatment Capone was receiving in Miami prompted him to seek refuge elsewhere in Florida. In June 1930, Capone purchased fifty-six acres in a remote section of Deerfield (now Deerfield Beach), Broward County. He planned to build a $250,000 estate on the property. His visions of a Florida mansion headquarters in Deerfield eventually fizzled out, and the property was sold. The area later became locally known as Capone Island. Today, the island property is known as Deerfield Island Park and is maintained by Broward County.

Although Capone was harassed and arrested many times in Florida, his money and lawyers always had the means to bail him out of jail. Florida had the same problems as Illinois, as it could not find a way to keep Capone in jail for his violations of the Volstead Act and many other violent and illegal activities.

In a twist of fate, the federal government turned to Capone's failure to pay income tax as a means to attempt to take the gangster off the streets and put him behind bars. In June 1931, Capone was indicted for federal income tax evasion.

When Capone's case was being prepared for trial, he was confident he would win by using his typical bribery and intimidation tactics. However, presiding federal judge James Wilkerson switched the entire jury pool after learning that Capone might have been able to bribe some members of the original jury pool. This ensured that the entire jury was not in the scope of Capone's influence.

On October 17, 1931, Capone was found guilty of three felony counts of tax evasion and two counts of failing to file a tax return (misdemeanors). He was sentenced to eleven years in federal prison, fined $50,000, charged $30,000 for court costs and ordered to pay $215,000 for back taxes plus interest. His lawyers filed an initial appeal, but it was denied, and the following rehearing of his appeal was also denied.

Capone's first two years in federal prison were spent in Atlanta in relative comfort, as he was bribing guards for preferential treatment.

In 1934, Capone's life in prison became difficult, as he was transferred to the notorious and isolated Alcatraz maximum-security federal penitentiary, which was located on the small (1.25 miles) Alcatraz Island off the coast of San Francisco, California. From its opening in 1934 until it closed in 1963, Alcatraz had the reputation as the toughest of all federal penitentiaries, and the facility incarcerated many of the nation's most dangerous felons, including George "Machine Gun" Kelly and Robert Stroud, the Birdman of Alcatraz.

While in Alcatraz, Capone was virtually cut off from his organized criminal empire. His health began to rapidly decline due to neurosyphilis (a bacterial infection of the brain or spinal cord, usually caused by the untreated sexually transmitted infectious disease syphilis). Capone also developed progressive dementia (loss of memory, language, problem-solving and other thinking abilities) due to neurosyphilis.

On January 6, 1939, Capone was released from Alcatraz due to his rapidly declining health and moved to Terminal Island in Los Angeles, California, to be treated by prison physicians.

On November 13, 1939, Capone was freed from federal prison and transported to the Union Memorial Hospital in Baltimore for additional treatment.

On March 19, 1940, Capone was released from the hospital in Baltimore, and he returned to his Palm Island, Florida house to live with his wife, Mae; son, Sonny; and Mae's brother Daniel Coughlin and his wife. Capone's life after prison was a mundane existence, as his mental and physical condition steadily worsened.

On January 25, 1947, he died in Florida from bronchopneumonia at the age of forty-eight.

When the *New York Times* reported Capone's death, the headlines read "End of an Evil Dream."

Eliot Ness versus Al Capone

Eliot Ness was a federal Prohibition agent known for his tireless labors to arrest and convict Al Capone. He worked with a handpicked team of incorruptible federal Prohibition agents known as "The Untouchables."

Ness was born on April 19, 1903, in Chicago, Illinois. He graduated from the University of Chicago in 1925, earning a degree in political science and business administration. In 1926, Ness became a federal Prohibition agent with the U.S. Treasury Department and was assigned to the Bureau of Prohibition in Chicago.

In 1930, President Herbert Hoover conceived a plan to form a small team of federal Prohibition agents to investigate Capone's illegal breweries, bootlegging operations, income tax evasion and other illicit activities. Ness was personally selected by U.S. attorney general William D. Mitchell to lead the team. Ness avoided corrupt agents by carefully selecting a team of six, which was later expanded to ten. Soon the team was called "The Untouchables."

Starting in March 1931, The Untouchables used surveillance, tips and wiretaps to raid Capone's empire of stills, breweries and warehouses. The team eventually destroyed or seized over $9 million of Capone's illicit property.

Later in 1931, Capone's syndicate attempted to bribe Ness with a payoff of $2,000 per week, but Ness refused to take the money and continued on his quest to bring Capone down. Other members of The Untouchables also refused to take bribes.

In June 1931, the work of The Untouchables led to Capone being indicted on five thousand violations of Prohibition laws. Judge James H. Wilkerson opted to have Capone charged on income tax evasion. Capone was found guilty of twenty-two counts of income tax evasion.

Reportedly, the only time Ness met Capone was on May 3, 1932, when he and other federal agents moved Capone from the Cook County Jail to Dearborn Station, where Capone was transferred by train to the Atlanta Federal Penitentiary.

After Prohibition was repealed, Ness worked in law enforcement; however, he was chastised for failing to solve the Cleveland Torso Murders (1935–38) and for attempting to cover up an accident he caused while driving drunk.

In 1944, Ness was hired as chairman of the Diebold Corporation in Ohio. In 1956, he started employment at the Guaranty Paper Corporation, which claimed it had a new anti-counterfeiting process for watermarking legal and official documents. This company crashed when it was disclosed that Ness's business partners were misrepresenting their process.

Ness was destitute for the remainder of his life and died on May 16, 1957, in Coudersport, Pennsylvania, at the age of fifty-four.

SEVERAL FLORIDA SHERIFFS AND POLITICIANS INDICTED

Bribery, corruption, neglect of duty and misconduct in public office were not uncommon in the state of Florida during Prohibition. There were scores of incidents in Florida during Prohibition that illuminate widespread corruption and misconduct by policemen, governmental officials, prominent citizens and politicians.

Indian River County sheriff Joel Knight was indicted by a circuit court grand jury and later sent to prison for accepting Prohibition-related bribes. On October 21, 1927, Knight was charged with five counts of bribery and two counts of malpractice while in office. The grand jury found that Sheriff Knight was accepting bribes from bootleggers and operators of gambling houses. The grand jury also recommended that Governor John W. Martin immediately remove Sheriff Knight from office for failure to enforce the laws of Indian River County.

Circuit court Judge Elwyn Thomas deputized City Marshal Eli Rymer to serve the arrest warrant on Sheriff Knight and fix the bond for his appearance in court. Sheriff Knight was removed from office, posted $12,000 bond and left Vero Beach pending a trial for the bribery charges in circuit court and another trial for malpractice in county court. Knight stated that "he was satisfied to leave his record in office to the citizens of the county. Indifference on the part of the public in observance of laws and failure of witnesses to disclose information they possessed when called to testify renders conviction of law violators difficult."

W.B. Davis, a former chief deputy under Knight, testified at Knight's circuit court trial that Sheriff Knight directed him to hijack a truck loaded with illicit liquor and deliver it to a garage operated by a bootlegger outfit south of Vero Beach.

Former Indian County sheriff Knight was convicted for conspiracy to violate Prohibition laws and was sentenced to thirteen months in U.S. prison and fined $500.

Most of the South Jacksonville city officials were indicted for violating the National Prohibition Act. On May 17, 1928, Francis L. Poor, chief assistant to United States attorney William Gober, announced that there were three groups of indictments: two charging conspiracy to violate the National Prohibition Act and a third charging illegal possession of liquor. Those who were indicted included William T. Harris, mayor; William P. Betloe, county commissioner; Paul C. Marion, president of the city council; Charles E.

Portrait of Indian River County sheriff Joel Knight. *From the* Miami Herald, *October 22, 1927.*

Steinhauser, chief of police; Rutledge Smith, chief of the fire department; Dwight W. Carpenter, assistant fire chief; J.M. Lorimer Jr. and J.M. Gray, city councilmen; J.M. Crary, former city engineer; and Asa B. Sands, discharged member of the police department. The two indictments charging conspiracy to violate the National Prohibition Act were charges of illegal transportation, possession and furnishing and delivering whiskey for beverage purposes. These were related to seven five-gallon jugs of liquor seized in June 1927.

On June 26, 1930, four South Jacksonville authorities and a civilian were convicted of conspiracy to violate the National Prohibition Act. Those convicted were Charles E. Steinhauser, chief of police; L.F. Jones, patrolman; Dwight W. Carpenter, assistant fire chief; J.M. Lorimer Jr., city councilman; and Abbott Simmons, civilian. Steinhauser was fined $230, and the other four were fined $100 each.

The Broward County sheriff and eight deputies were among thirty arrested for conspiracy to violate the National Prohibition Act. In January 1927, Broward County sheriff Paul O. Bryan, eight deputies and Broward County civilians were arrested by federal Prohibition agents. On November 24, 1928, Sheriff Bryan, eight deputies and several Fort Lauderdale police officers were fired. On December 6, 1928, a U.S. jury deadlocked in Miami after deliberating for more than forty hours, and another trial was scheduled.

The second trial on July 8, 1929, was held in U.S. district court in Miami and packed the courtroom with residents of the Fort Lauderdale area. U.S. district court Judge Halstead L. Ritter expressed his opinion to the jury before they deliberated. Judge Ritter said, "From the testimony of the witnesses in the court, it is my opinion that there were sufficient grounds to believe that there was a conspiracy among the defendants to violate the Prohibition laws." After eight hours of deliberation, the jury was unable to arrive at a decision on the case. Judge Ritter declared a mistrial with none of the defendants being convicted.

In 1912, former Seaboard Air Lines Railway train conductor W.H. "Ham" Dowling was elected as the Duval County sheriff. He was suspended by Florida governor Sidney Catts in 1917 for lax enforcement of the state's anti-liquor laws. He was reinstated a few months later. In 1923, Dowling was suspended by Florida governor Cary Hardee on a conspiracy charge but was once again reinstated. In 1928, Dowling was ousted as Duval County sheriff after losing the election to W.B. Cahoon, who ran his campaign promising to bring tough enforcement to Jacksonville.

In 1930, Dowling was arrested for possessing and operating two stills, 14,000 gallons of beer, 250 gallons of whiskey and 79 bottles of moonshine. Dowling tried to talk his way out of trouble by claiming he did not know the illegal distilling equipment and alcohol were on his property. Unfortunately for the former county sheriff, he was convicted of violating Prohibition laws in 1931 and sentenced to serve two years in the Atlanta federal prison.

"When Prohibition was introduced, I hoped that it would be widely supported by public opinion and the day would soon come when the evil effects of alcohol would be recognized. I have slowly and reluctantly come to believe that this has not been the result. Instead, drinking has generally increased; the speakeasy has replaced the saloon; a vast army of lawbreakers has appeared; many of our best citizens have openly ignored Prohibition; respect for the law has been greatly lessened; and crime has increased to a level never seen before."

–John D. Rockefeller

The Increased Penalties Act

On March 2, 1929, President Calvin Coolidge signed the Increased Penalties Act (also called the Jones-Stalker Act or the Jones Act) into law. Its purpose was to strengthen the penalties for people who were convicted of violating Prohibition laws for commercial purposes. The Volstead Act provided lesser penalties for the importation or transportation of illicit liquor compared to stiffer penalties for the manufacture or sale. The act stated that any violation of the Volstead Act (manufacture, sale, transportation, importation or exportation of illicit liquor) would have a penalty of a fine not to exceed $10,000 or imprisonment not to exceed five years, or both. The intent of Congress was to ensure that the courts "should discriminate between casual or slight violations and habitual sales of intoxicating liquor, or attempts to commercialize violations of the law" and sentence offenders accordingly.

Chapter 5

RUMRUNNING IN FLORIDA

Rumrunning is defined as the illicit transportation and smuggling of alcoholic beverages over water. Rumrunning first appeared as a term around 1916, but it soon became synonymous with Prohibition as ships began transporting rum from the Caribbean islands into Florida. With 1,350 miles of coastline, not counting its many bays, inlets and barrier islands, Florida was a difficult place for federal agents to enforce Prohibition laws. Additionally, with Florida's proximity to many Caribbean islands, the state was a logical place to set up operations for alcohol smuggling activities.

Smugglers realized that rum was not as profitable as other alcoholic beverages such as Canadian whiskey, English gin, French champagne and scotch. Soon after Prohibition began, many types of alcoholic beverages were being smuggled into the United States aboard ships, and rumrunning evolved into a term used for the water-based smuggling of any type of illicit liquor.

Many of the nations in the Caribbean islands (some of which were havens for pirates during the Golden Age of Piracy in the late seventeenth and early eighteenth centuries) became a mecca for rumrunners during Prohibition. The importation of Canadian and European liquor was increased as their customs revenues expanded, and many new jobs were created.

In 1921, the Bahamas improved their main harbors, using liquor revenues to expand their liquor traffic capabilities. The majority of this imported liquor eventually found its way from the Caribbean islands into the United States via rumrunners.

At the beginning of Prohibition, the U.S. Coast Guard was not prepared to deal with the increase of smuggling operations. They were understaffed and undertrained and did not possess enough boats and ships to stop most of the rumrunners. In fact, their fastest boats had a top speed of only twelve knots (about fourteen miles per hour). Realizing this deficiency in U.S. Coast Guard capabilities, some rumrunners began using large cargo boats with shallow drafts equipped with 450-horsepower Liberty aircraft engines. They were primarily built in boat yards in south Florida. The vessels became known as "Bimini boats" and could easily outrun the swiftest of U.S. Coast Guard boats during the early years of Prohibition. These Bimini boats could also maneuver around in Florida's mangrove swamps and narrow inlets, places where the U.S. Coast Guard boats were unable to venture and where many smuggling debarkation points were located.

Oftentimes, rumrunners would hire local fishermen to act as lookouts for the U.S. Coast Guard to ensure their cargos of illicit liquor would make it to land, where they could be safely unloaded and transferred onto cars and trucks. Much of this illicit liquor was shipped out of Florida, and many times it was packed in cases labeled as fish, citrus fruit, vegetables, bottled goods and household commodities.

Some of the rumrunners' tricks of the trade used to help them avoid arrest were to build concealed sections in their boats to hide liquor bottles, build double or false bottoms, falsely label liquor crates and mix liquor bottles with legitimate goods. Another notable innovation was the use of a submersion tank, which was a long, cigar-shaped metal container that was chained underneath the ship and was not visible from the surface. These submersion tanks would be cut loose, usually at night, and towed ashore by contact boats (small high-speed vessels used for smuggling operations). If the U.S. Coast Guard spotted a contact boat that was towing a submersion tank, the rumrunners would usually release it so it would sink to avoid seizure.

U.S. officials did not anticipate the extent of nonsupport for the enforcement of Prohibition laws by foreign governments, although there were a few indications before the Eighteenth Amendment was enacted. The major problem was with Great Britain, as its officials allowed their Caribbean colonies, including the Bahamas, to engage in smuggling operations into the United States. Diplomacy between Great Britain and the United States became tense.

Florida senator Park Trammell contacted U.S. secretary of state Charles Hughes and called for a treaty with Great Britain that would prohibit that nation's ships from transporting alcoholic beverages into the United States.

On January 23, 1924, the United States and Great Britain signed the Anglo-American liquor treaty. The terms of the treaty gave the United States a considerable advantage in combating rumrunning. The United States was now authorized to board ships that were suspected of rumrunning and flying the British flag within one hour's sailing distance from U.S. territory. U.S. authorities could now question anyone on board the ship and inspect the ship's documentation. If there was a "reasonable cause for belief" that the ship was in violation of U.S. Prohibition laws, it could be seized and escorted or towed into a U.S. port for further investigation under U.S. law.

The United States agreed to allow British ships carrying a cargo of liquor destined for foreign ports to stop at U.S. ports as long as the liquor remained sealed and was not unloaded. Similar treaties with several other nations were also signed.

BILL MCCOY ("THE REAL MCCOY") AND RUM ROW

William Frederick "Bill" McCoy was born in Syracuse, New York, on August 17, 1877. His father, William, served in the Union navy during the American Civil War and participated in blockading major ports of the Confederacy. McCoy chose a life at sea and was trained aboard the school ship USS *Saratoga* and graduated first in his class from the Pennsylvania Nautical School in 1895. He spent the next few years serving as mate and quartermaster on various ships, including the SS *Olivette*.

Around 1900, the McCoy family moved to Holly Hill, Florida. Bill and his older brother Ben went into the boat yard and taxi boat service businesses in Holly Hill and Jacksonville. They built large shallow-draft power yachts for many of the nation's wealthiest families and gained a good business reputation.

Around 1918, Bill and Ben McCoy found themselves in financial trouble due to failed investments in the freight business. When Prohibition went into effect in 1920, Bill, a lifelong teetotaler, believed the law was an absurd infringement on personal rights. The brothers were propositioned by a rumrunner to sail an illicit shipment of liquor into the United States from international waters. They initially declined, but the brothers had second thoughts due to their financial predicament and decided to try their luck in the potentially lucrative, but dangerous, rumrunning occupation.

Rumrunner Captain William F. "Bill" McCoy, circa 1921. *Courtesy of the Halifax Historical Museum, Daytona Beach—photograph by author.*

Above, left: Barometer from Bill McCoy's *Henry L. Marshall* ship. *Courtesy of the Halifax Historical Museum, Daytona Beach—photograph by author.*

Above, right: Binoculars once owned by Bill McCoy. *Courtesy of the Halifax Historical Museum, Daytona Beach—photograph by author.*

In early 1921, the McCoys gathered up their savings and purchased a ninety-foot schooner named the *Henry L. Marshall.* Bill McCoy sailed to the port of Nassau and purchased 1,500 cases of Canadian whiskey. He smuggled it into the United States at St. Catherine's Sound and sold it for $15,000, making a huge profit.

During Prohibition, a line of ships loaded with liquor anchored beyond the maritime limit of the United States (three miles prior to April 21, 1924, and twelve miles thereafter), and this became known as Rum Row. Rumrunners would sell alcoholic beverages to smugglers from their anchored freight ships at Rum Row. The smugglers would then illegally sneak into U.S. ports and resell their illicit alcohol cargo, usually pocketing excellent profits. This lucrative smuggling business had many dangers, as violent crimes including hijackings and murder were not uncommon.

In the beginning of Prohibition, Rum Row was initially established off the coast of Florida, where rum was smuggled in from the Caribbean. As the smuggling of Canadian and European liquor increased, Rum Row locations were extended to all coastlines of the United States. By far the busiest was the coast of New Jersey.

McCoy is often credited as the originator of Rum Row. He used his familiarity with domestic maritime laws and experience as a mariner to pioneer rumrunning operations. He documented the *Henry L. Marshall* schooner under a British flag and established his company in Halifax, Nova Scotia, Canada. He also had official British documents written that declared his ship was transporting legal liquor from one non-U.S. port to another. As long as McCoy operated in international waters, he was outside the reach of U.S. jurisdiction.

McCoy forged a few basic rules that made him a successful rumrunner: "Stay true to your contract, stay clear of the government's notice, stay well offshore, and stay vigilant to avoid Coast Guard cutters."

In only a few years, McCoy became the most notorious rumrunner of them all. U.S. and international press dubbed him "Rummy McCoy," and he became a household name and an international celebrity.

"The Real McCoy"

Bill McCoy earned the nickname of the "Real McCoy" during Prohibition. The term is an idiom and metaphor that evolved to mean "the real thing" or "the genuine article." It most likely originated from the phrase "The Real MacKay," which appeared in a Scottish poem in 1856. Reportedly, it was later refashioned into the term the "Real McCoy."

Bill McCoy ran his rumrunning operations very honestly and sold liquor in original sealed factory bottles and unadulterated. This is most likely how his nickname of the "Real McCoy" originated.

"Smugglers Ham"

McCoy was not just known for the founding of Rum Row; he also reportedly developed the creative method of storing, moving and transporting liquor bottles aboard vessels known as smugglers ham. Smugglers and the U.S. Coast Guard also called this method "burlock." This smuggling method arranged six bottles in a pyramid shape and tightly wrapped them in straw and burlap: three on the bottom, two in the middle and one on the top. The smugglers ham method allowed bundles to be neatly stacked top to bottom, able to withstand rough handling, and made loading, transporting and unloading from vessels much easier and more efficient. The bundles also took up about one-third the space of the standard wooden cases, which typically held a dozen bottles. As a precaution to being caught with illicit liquor, some rumrunners added salt into the smugglers ham bundles. If a rumrunning vessel was spotted by law enforcement, the bundles would be thrown overboard and would sink out of sight below the surface. When the salt eventually dissolved, the smugglers ham bundles would float back to the surface, and the rumrunners could retrieve their illicit cargo.

The Tomoka *Seized by the U.S. Coast Guard*

The McCoy brothers decided to purchase a large schooner capable of transporting five thousand cases of liquor with a combination of rumrunning profits and a loan from gangsters they were acquainted with. The schooner was renamed from the *Arethusa* to the *Tomoka* and became Bill McCoy's favorite ship.

McCoy appointed Carl Anderson, his former first mate, captain of the *Henry L. Marshall.* Before McCoy sailed away aboard the *Tomoka* on his own rumrunning adventures, he handed written instructions to Anderson for a delivery of 1,500 cases of liquor off the coast of Atlantic City, New Jersey. Captain Anderson decided to break McCoy's instructions and rules and sell the liquor for a higher price. Soon afterward, Anderson disclosed many of McCoy's rumrunning secrets to a reporter while onboard the *Henry L. Marshall.*

These leaked McCoy rumrunning trade secrets caught the attention of the U.S. Coast Guard, and they sent the cutter *Seneca* (CG-85) to investigate the activities of the *Henry L. Marshall.* The *Seneca* sighted a vessel flying a British flag that fit the *Henry L. Marshall*'s description and assumed the schooner engaged in illegal exchanges with contact boats from the United States. Although the *Henry L. Marshall* was in international waters, the U.S. Coast Guard claimed this constituted an illegal act. The *Seneca* reported its position as five miles off Little Egg Inlet, which was outside U.S. territorial waters, but still launched a boat with a boarding team. Even though the *Henry L. Marshall* was beyond U.S. jurisdiction, the Coast Guard had legal authority to board it because they suspected illegal activities, which violated U.S. law. After boarding the schooner, the Coast Guard revealed that the schooner was concealing its name and home port under canvas covers.

The U.S. Coast Guard's boarding team discovered that the vessel was the *Henry L. Marshall* and its home port was Nassau. The vessel was also carrying 1,250 cases of scotch whiskey. Since there was no legal documentation authorizing the transfer of the *Henry L. Marshall*'s flag to Great Britain, the Coast Guard had adequate justification to seize the vessel.

After the *Henry L. Marshall* was escorted into New York, the Coast Guard discovered documentation that had fraudulently allowed it to enter into U.S. ports after delivering its illicit cargo. McCoy's handwritten instructions to Captain Anderson were also discovered, which identified him as the owner of the *Henry L. Marshall* and the mastermind of its rumrunning operations.

The confiscation of the *Henry L. Marshall* was the first major seizure of a rumrunning vessel by the U.S. Coast Guard during Prohibition.

Prohibition enforcement agents promptly arrested the *Henry L. Marshall*'s captain, Carl Anderson, and its first mate, C. Thompson. Federal warrants were issued for John G. Crossland, the broker of the illicit liquor operation, and Bill McCoy, the owner of the *Henry L. Marshall*. Federal agents quickly arrested Crossland, but McCoy was somewhere on the high seas and was able to elude arrest. Bill McCoy was now a fugitive and the focus of an intensive U.S. law enforcement manhunt.

The Federal Government's Main Target

McCoy's celebrity grew as he was making a mockery of the inept ability of the U.S. Coast Guard to capture him. It was reported that his rumrunning operation expanded to five boats with dozens of crew members.

Mabel Walker Willebrandt, the young and highly motivated U.S. assistant attorney general, set goals to arrest the now famous rumrunner Bill McCoy, who was embarrassing the federal government with his elusive high seas smuggling exploits.

Willebrandt considered Bill McCoy to be the federal government's main target (the precursor to Public Enemy Number One). She encouraged the U.S. Coast Guard to hunt him down with the backing of a new treaty with Great Britain that allowed the United States to board British ships in international waters if they were suspected of rumrunning into the United States.

McCoy the Lifesaver

A federal agent named Peter J. Sullivan was sent on an undercover mission to Nassau, Bahamas, to obtain information about rumrunners, including Bill McCoy. A group of unscrupulous rumrunners and mobsters discovered Sullivan's identity and made plans to murder him. When McCoy heard of the plans to murder Sullivan, he became determined to prevent their ruthless plot. He invited Sullivan to hide out overnight in his hotel. The next morning, McCoy smuggled him onto a ferry bound for Miami, out of harm's way. McCoy's moral code did not include murder. This honorable good deed helped define McCoy's decent moral character for the rest of his life.

McCoy Outgunned and Arrested

McCoy's legendary high seas rumrunning adventures came to an end on November 23, 1923, when the U.S. Coast Guard boarded his British registered ship *Tomoka* in international waters off the coast of Sea Bright, New Jersey. Coast Guard lieutenant Perkins ordered McCoy to sail the *Tomoka* to Sandy Hook, Connecticut, as he claimed that the *Tomoka*'s documents were not legal. McCoy refused the orders and promptly sailed the *Tomoka* farther out into international waters.

The *Seneca* was under orders to seize the *Tomoka* or sink it. The *Seneca* pursued McCoy and the *Tomoka* for several miles and then fired a shell over the *Tomoka*'s bow. The *Tomoka* returned machine gun fire, but McCoy realized that the *Seneca*'s military-grade four-inch shells were too powerful to contend with. McCoy brought the *Tomoka* to a stop and surrendered. The U.S. Coast Guard arrested McCoy and his crew and seized the *Tomoka*. The *Tomoka* was carrying around four hundred cases of whiskey, and McCoy had more than $60,000 in cash on board the vessel. As the *Tomoka* was being escorted to Sandy Hook, McCoy paid his crew their wages and wished them all good luck, as he realized his rumrunning days were likely over.

McCoy's Legal Battle and Light Prison Sentence

McCoy claimed he was not breaking any U.S. laws. As he told reporters, "I was outside the three-mile limit, selling whisky, and good whisky, to anyone and everyone who wanted to buy." However, the treaty with Great

Britain proved to be the catalyst that led to his downfall as the most famous rumrunner in U.S. history.

Mabel Walker Willebrandt offered McCoy a deal of leniency if he would cooperate with the Justice Department. McCoy pleaded guilty, but only after he was able to negotiate the charges being dropped against his brother and was not required to testify against any other rumrunners.

In March 1925, Bill McCoy was sentenced to serve only nine months in prison at the Essex County Jail in New Jersey. This was the result of almost two years of costly legal maneuvering. McCoy reportedly lost a lot of his wealth and all of his ships. However, his celebrity status accompanied him to jail. Prison officials allowed him to occasionally leave the jailhouse as long as he returned by 9:00 p.m. While McCoy was incarcerated, Charles E. Blue, the warden of the prison, accompanied him to the Walker-Shade prizefight at Ebbets Field in Brooklyn. Photographs appeared on the front page of newspapers showing Blue and McCoy sitting together in ringside seats. The warden was fired, and McCoy was denied an early release from prison.

Bill McCoy Returns to Civilian Life

Bill McCoy was released from prison on Christmas Day 1925 after serving his full nine-month sentence. His brother Ben picked him up at the prison, and they drove back to Florida, discussing what their next business adventures would be. The McCoys decided that the rumrunning business was too dangerous to reenter, as the U.S. Coast Guard's patrols were now more efficient. Additionally, ruthless hijacking and piracy on the high seas had escalated, and organized crime had taken over the majority of the illicit trade. No reports ever surfaced that indicated the McCoy brothers ventured back into the rumrunning business.

Instead, the McCoy brothers decided to live modestly in Holly Hill, Florida, and they returned to the legitimate boatbuilding business and ventured into real estate investments. Over the years, they also donated their time, money and skills to restoring several important historical ships.

In 1929, the *Arethusa* (*Tomoka*), McCoy's once-prized possession, wrecked during a snowstorm at the entrance of Halifax Harbor in Nova Scotia, Canada. After McCoy was initially arrested, the U.S. Coast Guard had impounded the schooner. It was later auctioned off and wound up being used in the fishing trade in Nova Scotia. McCoy had lost track of it after his

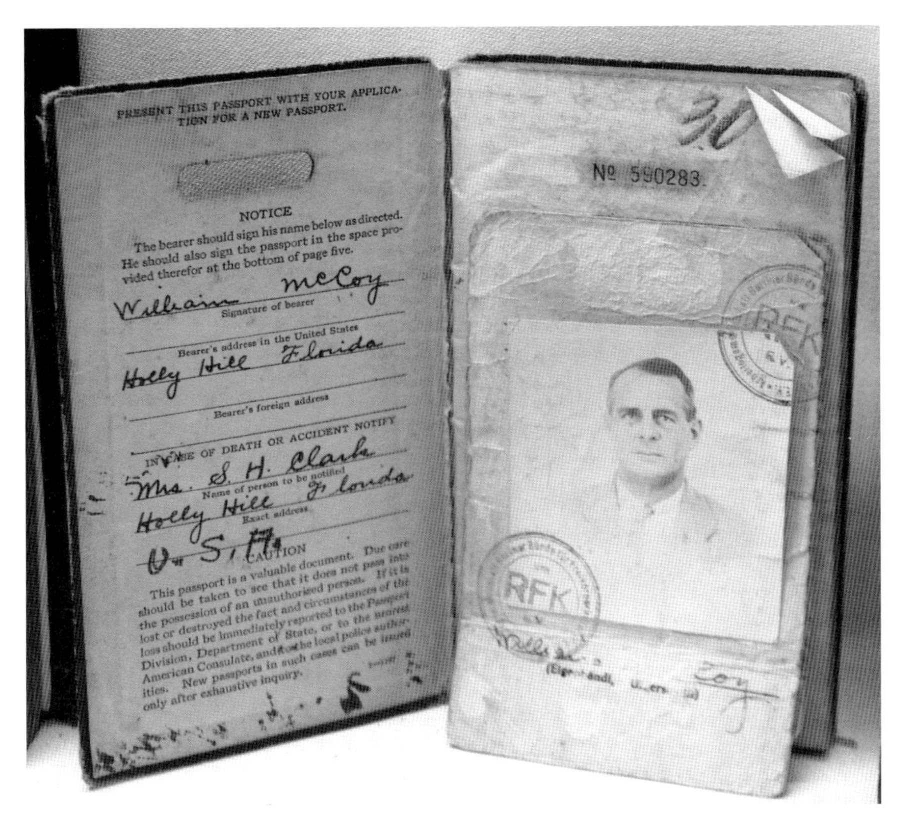

Bill McCoy's passport with his United States address listed as Holly Hill, Florida. *Courtesy of the Halifax Historical Museum, Daytona Beach—photograph by author.*

arrest. He anxiously traveled to Canada to discover what remained of it and to find out if it was salvageable. McCoy was led to some of the schooner's wreckage and realized it was a total loss. He salvaged several pieces and donated them to various museums. The *Arethusa*'s plans are housed in the Smithsonian Institution, and the ship is an important piece of maritime folklore to this day.

Bill McCoy's Legacy

On December 30, 1948, Bill McCoy, the legendary pioneer rumrunner of the Prohibition era, died of a heart attack and complications of food poisoning aboard his ship *Blue Lagoon* in Stuart, Florida. He was seventy-one years old.

McCoy claimed he never paid a cent to organized crime, corrupt politicians or crooked law enforcement personnel for bribes or protection as he transported an estimated two million bottles of liquor during his infamously short-lived rumrunning career.

Bill McCoy was the national symbol for defiance of Prohibition, which is still considered to be the most unpopular law in U.S. history. Since he always operated in international waters, he always believed he was not breaking any U.S. laws.

Many believe that McCoy was the catalyst for the development of the modern U.S. Coast Guard due to his innovative rumrunning methods, especially the invention of Rum Row. As a result, the U.S. Coast Guard was forced to expand personnel, training and its ship and boat fleet.

McCoy maintained the character of a gentleman although he dealt with many unscrupulous characters in the illicit liquor business. He was respected as he transacted honest business deals and was actually considered an honorable outlaw by a large percentage of the general public.

The term "The Real McCoy" was used before Bill McCoy became famous during the days of Prohibition. However, the term has evolved to mean "the real thing" or "the genuine article" thanks to McCoy's insistence on selling authentic alcoholic beverages in their original factory-sealed bottles.

Prohibition's Lady Rumrunners

The 1920s was a decade that marked significant progress for the empowerment of women. The WCTU was the catalyst that forced the issue of alcohol control into the national spotlight. On August 18, 1920, the Nineteenth Amendment granted women the right to vote. Prohibition brought women out of the shadows, and their homes, and allowed them the freedom to drink alcohol in speakeasies, smoke in public, cut their hair in trendy bob styles and wear sleeveless gowns and short skirts. Opportunities for women expanded in legitimate and illegitimate arenas.

It is certainly true that men dominated the illicit rumrunning trade during the Prohibition era; however, some women were prominently involved as well. Two of the most successful rumrunners were women, and they both played a noteworthy role in Florida's Prohibition history. Their names are Gertrude "Cleo" Lythgoe and Marie Waite.

"The Queen of the Bahamas"/"The Queen of Rum Row"

Arguably, the most famous female rumrunner was Gertrude "Cleo" Lythgoe, also named the "Queen of the Bahamas" or the "Queen of Rum Row." She was said to look like the Egyptian pharaoh Cleopatra, hence the nickname of "Cleo."

Prior to Prohibition, she was employed at Williams and Company, a London liquor exporter. When Prohibition became the law of the land, the London liquor exporter decided to illegally supply liquor into the United States via the Bahamas. Lythgoe set up the company's wholesale liquor business in the Bahamas and was the only woman to hold such a license during the Prohibition years. She also managed rumrunning operations and became an intimidating figure in the liquor supply business despite her sex.

During her three-year rumrunning career, she was shipwrecked twice, shot at many times, pursued by ruthless pirates, suspected of being a spy, hunted by federal Prohibition agents, kidnapped, had her life threatened by several competitors and arrested.

Lythgoe became lifelong friends with Bill McCoy after sailing with him on board his schooner *Tomoka* for several weeks selling her company's liquor, a highly sought-after cargo of genuine American rye, from Rum Row. Lythgoe purchased the rye for $7 a case and it sold for $60 a case. McCoy paid her with $1,000 bills.

Lythgoe became somewhat of a celebrity as reporters followed her to the Bahamas, a book was written about her and the *New York Times* began running weekly features about her.

Lythgoe's rumrunning career was halted after she was arrested and charged with smuggling one thousand cases of liquor into New Orleans. She was acquitted in federal court when it was proven she was not involved with that particular shipment of illicit liquor.

In 1926, she closed down her office in the Bahamas and moved to Detroit, where she opened a rental car company. After more than twenty years in the rental car business, she sold out and moved to Miami.

On June 24, 1974, after losing much of her wealth due to failed investments, she died in relative obscurity in Los Angeles at the age of eighty-six.

"Personally I do not feel that I have acted wrongly any more than a hardware dealer or a manufacturer of firearms might if he were charged with 'abetting crime.'"
–Gertrude "Cleo" Lythgoe

"SPANISH MARIE"

Around 1924, Charlie Waite and his wife, Marie, later to be known as "Spanish Marie," opened the Miami Academy of Dance, a front for a rumrunning business. Charlie became known around Florida as the "King of the Rumrunners," as he was successfully smuggling large quantities of liquor into Florida from the Bahamas and Cuba.

In 1927, Charlie and two of his crew were arrested by the U.S. Coast Guard. They attempted to escape, and a shootout broke out, resulting in the death of two of them, including Charlie, who fell overboard into Biscayne Bay. His body was never recovered. Marie Waite took over the family's rumrunning business and expanded it to include fifteen boats operating in the Straits of Florida. She was soon commonly referred to as Spanish Marie.

Before the U.S. Coast Guard was equipped with faster ships, Spanish Marie smuggled liquor in groups of four boats that were capable of outrunning Coast Guard vessels. Three carried the liquor cargo, and the fourth was armed. If Spanish Marie's ships were spotted, the armed ship would engage the U.S. Coast Guard as the three liquor cargo–carrying ships would speed away to Miami or Key West.

When the U.S. Coast Guard received faster ships, Spanish Marie changed her rumrunning strategy to have her crews and ships equipped with radios. She then had a pirate radio transmitter installed in Key West to ensure the U.S. Coast Guard had clear reception of her broadcasts. She created a secret set of codes to relay instructions to her rumrunning crews. She also provided false information over radio transmissions that kept her rumrunning operation from being infiltrated by federal agents and the U.S. Coast Guard.

On March 12, 1928, after the federal government cracked her secret code, she received a phone call stating that a liquor cargo from Bimini had safely arrived in Coconut Grove. She left her two small children in their Miami home and drove to Coconut Grove to supervise the unloading and distribution of the illicit liquor. It was a trap by the U.S. Coast Guard, and Spanish Marie was arrested on the beach in Coconut Grove as the illicit liquor was being unloaded from her boat *Kid Boots*.

After her arrest, Spanish Marie pleaded with the federal authorities that she had to return home to her small children. She was released on $500 bail with the stipulation she would appear in court the following day. The next day, her attorney showed up and stated that Spanish Marie was suffering from mental trauma and could not travel to the courthouse. The judge then increased her bond to $3,000.

Spanish Marie disappeared with her boats and a reported $1 million. She was never convicted of Prohibition violations.

The Rum War and Demise of Rum Row

During Prohibition, the U.S. Coast Guard was in charge of suppressing illegal liquor traffic into the United States from sea. The battles between rumrunners and the U.S. Coast Guard are known as "The Rum War." From the onset of Prohibition, the U.S. Coast Guard was under immense pressure from the drys to squelch the illegal importation of liquor from the seas. The U.S. Coast Guard had other important duties in addition to the enforcement of Prohibition, including its search-and-rescue duties and lifesaving missions. The enforcement of Prohibition laws stretched the U.S. Coast Guard's resources thin and limited the effectiveness of this service branch.

From 1920 to 1925, the U.S. Coast Guard was not equipped to adequately stop most rumrunning operations. During this period, the U.S. Coast Guard's resources remained at almost the same level as 1920, despite a significant increase in the amount of illicit alcohol that was being smuggled into the United States. Statistics regarding the amount of illicit liquor entering the United States during this time are impossible to calculate; however, one indicator is the amount of liquor passing through Nassau, Bahamas, into the United States, which was fifty thousand quarts in 1917 compared to ten million quarts in 1922.

As illicit liquor profits soared, sophisticated criminal syndicates invested in faster boats and initiated more violence on the high seas. These factors further jeopardized the U.S. Coast Guard's ability to apprehend rumrunners.

In 1924, President Calvin Coolidge appropriated nearly $14 million in funding for the U.S. Coast Guard. Current boats were updated, and new boats were purchased. New U.S. Coast Guard stations were built in Florida in Fernandina and St. Petersburg, which supplemented the existing stations in Fort Lauderdale, Miami and Key West.

After 1925, the U.S. Coast Guard's effectiveness in enforcing Prohibition drastically improved as more equipment, men and ships became operational. Between 1924 and 1926, U.S. Coast Guard personnel levels jumped almost 50 percent, from 5,982 to 10,009.

The U.S. Coast Guard was now able to initiate more aggressive tactics to combat rumrunners. Additionally, the United States signed multiple maritime agreements with various nations, including Canada, Mexico, Great Britain and France, that allowed suspected rumrunning ships to be seized in international waters.

The maritime limit of the United States was increased to twelve miles on April 21, 1924, and this was technically an hour's steaming distance from the shoreline. Foreign ships were now liable to seizure if they were in contact with any U.S. ship within this distance. This drastically cut down on the number of small contact boats making trips to Rum Row.

Improved radio direction technology allowed two U.S. Coast Guard cutters working together to intercept transmissions from rumrunning ships and establish their location.

Throughout the Prohibition era, the slow speed of U.S. Coast Guard ships was highly criticized in the press. However, the U.S. Coast Guard stated that speed was not its highest priority, as the larger, and slower, rumrunning supply ships were their targets. The U.S. Coast Guard used long-range seaworthy vessels to run down many of their prime targets.

All of these factors allowed the U.S. Coast Guard to get the upper hand in the Rum War. The amount of rumrunning activity at Rum Row drastically declined as the U.S. Coast Guard was responsible for seizing literally thousands of vessels during Prohibition.

Florida Begins Using Seaplanes against Rumrunners

On April 16, 1926, Philip F. Hambsch, a Florida Prohibition administrator, learned at a conference of dry agents in Savannah, Georgia, that many rumrunners were moving their operations southward from New York and New Jersey. Hambsch said, "Most of the rum runners have discontinued their trade out of Long Island and are now coming south for the illicit sale of their liquors….The reason for this is easy to understand. Both the Coast Guard and Prohibition forces have made rum running around New York virtually impossible by their careful watch of the coast. We are preparing to meet these rum runners."

U.S. Navy–type seaplanes with speeds of ninety miles per hour carrying machine guns were deployed as a blockade off the coasts of Florida, Georgia, North Carolina and South Carolina. Florida started with four of these seaplanes off the coast of Pensacola and increased the number of federal Prohibition agents to assist with the new strategy against rumrunners. The seaplanes flew night and day and proved fairly effective in combating rumrunning activity.

Chapter 6

BOOTLEGGING AND MOONSHINING IN FLORIDA

Bootlegging is defined as the illicit production, selling and smuggling of alcoholic beverages over land. Moonshining is defined as the illicit production of high-proof distilled alcoholic beverages. Bathtub gin is defined as homemade poor-quality alcoholic beverages made from cheap grain alcohol, water and various flavoring agents.

One of the main issues with the enforcement of Prohibition laws was the ease, and relative low cost, to distill homemade alcohol. Many Floridians in the state's rural interior made moonshine, beer and other bootleg liquor and sold it to make extra cash.

After Prohibition began and forced the closure of most legal breweries, some survived in business by brewing "near beer" (beer with less than 0.5 percent alcohol by volume). Others survived by making malt extract (a weak alcoholic preparation derived from starch or grain that is similar to beer but thicker in consistency and darker in color). This malt extract was sold to consumers as a cooking product along with instructions on how to use it to make bread, the "light and perfectly browned" type. This was the "not-so-secret" recipe to brew your own beer.

Some of the major breweries survived through Prohibition by making products other than beer: Anheuser-Busch (ice cream and soft drinks), Coors (glassware and all types of ceramic dinnerware), Hamm's (near beer), Miller (near beer), Pabst (cheese), Schlitz (chocolate), Stroh's (ice cream and malt extract) and Yuengling (near beer and ice cream).

Confiscated moonshine laid about on a residential street in DeLand, Florida, circa 1922. *Courtesy of State Archives of Florida.*

Some hardware stores advertised and sold parts required for building stills. Libraries kept books on their shelves that included instructions to build stills and brew homemade beer.

Prohibition provided the reason for many people to become proficient in making their own alcoholic beverages. This was one of the contributing reasons that tens of thousands of normally law-abiding citizens became lawbreakers during Prohibition.

Between 1919 and 1929, the sales of corn sugar, the basic component of corn whiskey, increased six times, indicating a rapid increase of illicit still operations.

The Dixie Highway, a connected network of paved roads constructed from 1915 to 1929 that ran from Michigan to Miami and included east, central and west routes through Florida, became one of the main bootlegging roadways throughout the Prohibition era.

State, local and federal authorities, to some extent, attempted to enforce the Prohibition laws, but they were never able to fully stamp out illegal alcohol activities in Florida. Florida's dense wilderness and remote swamps served as some of the more ideal hideouts for bootlegging operations and moonshine stills.

Not long after Prohibition became the law of the land, Florida became known as "Bootleggers Paradise." Florida was also called the "leakiest place in the country."

STAYING ONE STEP AHEAD OF THE LAW

Bootleggers went to some extraordinary measures to stay one step ahead of the law. Liquor and moonshine bottles were often disguised in boxes and crates labeled as cakes, choice meats, citrus fruits, cookies, fresh fish, pastries and pies in an attempt to avoid detection. One of the more interesting tricks that bootleggers used during Prohibition was the use of cow shoes.

Cow shoes were designed so if law enforcement agents and officers found the tracks of an animal such as a horse or cow and no human footprints, they would not investigate the area and any illegal stills hidden would not be discovered.

A July 21, 1924 article in the *Palm Beach Post* describes how this deception worked until law enforcement became wise to it:

> *Here is the newest way to try to outwit Prohibition agents. Just put on a pair of "cow shoes" if the dry boys get on your trail. They fooled the*

"Cow shoes" were used during Prohibition to hide human footprints. *Courtesy of the Library of Congress.*

agents down around Hillsboro, Fla.—for a little while. Running across a large still, the agents started hunting the operator. He was nowhere in sight. And no human footprints could be seen. But there were marks of bovine hoofs. The agents followed them and found the distiller. One look at his shoes convinced them the footprints were his. Two blocks of wood, cut to resemble a cow's hoofs, were fastened to a wire frame attached to the soles of his shoes.

The Prevalence of Bootlegging and Moonshining in Florida

Throughout the years of Prohibition, an untold number of bootleggers and moonshiners were operating around the state of Florida. Arrests and police raids were common, which demonstrate that illegal alcohol production and trafficking were prolific in Florida. Illegal stills were not just located in remote wilderness and swampy areas. Some were operating in attics, garages, basements, kitchens and commercial buildings. Stills operating in residential and populated areas were a public hazard, as they had the potential to explode and cause fires. Following are some Florida stories of bootlegging and moonshining escapades, police raids, arrests, confiscations, crook-versus-crook, speakeasies and the smashing of illegal still equipment by law enforcement.

Jacksonville

During the 1920s, Jacksonville was known as the "Gateway to Florida" because the major roads and train routes connected through the city. Jacksonville's harbors were known for rumrunning, and its streets had plenty of bootleggers trafficking illegal alcohol to speakeasies and thirsty citizens. The city has its share of provocative Prohibition stories in addition to Al Capone staying in the Casa Marina Hotel in the late 1920s and visiting the Hysler crime syndicate family ("Whiskey King of Jacksonville") in March 1930.

A yard in Jacksonville was irrigated with moonshine when resident Glenn Robinson buried twenty-five barrels containing mash whiskey and connected them with iron siphoning pipes. Robinson was making moonshine on his farm with a copper still that had the capacity of one hundred gallons per day.

Confiscated gambling equipment and a still that was used to make illicit moonshine and liquor in Jacksonville, Florida, circa 1925. *Courtesy of State Archives of Florida.*

Dry agents dug up the barrels, confiscated the stash of moonshine and the still and arrested Robinson for violation of Prohibition laws. Jacksonville's underground moonshining operation was foiled.

The Jacksonville Brewing Company was founded by German immigrant William Ostner in 1913 and opened in 1914 on West Sixteenth Street. The company's flagship product was a German pilsner called Jax Beer. During Prohibition, the company changed its operations from brewing beer to cold storage and changed its name to the Jacksonville Cold Storage Company. Within weeks after the repeal of Prohibition, beer was being produced once again. Reportedly, William Oster came up with the idea to sell beer six to a sack. The idea caught on throughout the beer industry, and Oster is oftentimes referred to as the "Father of the Six-Pack."

On June 13, 1926, Adolphus Ward, a Jacksonville mail carrier and alleged bootlegger, was shot on a residential street and died a week later. Mrs. Lyndall MacMurray was arrested in Nashville for his murder and brought back to Jacksonville to stand trial. Ward was apparently mistreating MacMurray after she stole ten cases of whiskey from him, and this was identified as the motive for the murder. MacMurray was known as a Main Street vendor who sold soda from the front of a tent and illicit whiskey behind the tent. MacMurray became somewhat of a Prohibition celebrity among women, and the courthouse was packed with women during her trial. MacMurray claimed she shot Ward to protect her fourteen-year-old son, John, and herself. After the jury deliberated for only forty minutes, they came back with a verdict of "not guilty."

Key West

During Prohibition, Key West was a mecca for rumrunning, and illicit liquor was easy to find. Many speakeasies were established in Key West, and the working-class city became known for its widespread wet reputation and lax enforcement of Prohibition laws. It was reported that Key West's law enforcement and governmental officials not only looked the other way, but many were allegedly involved in the illicit liquor trade as well.

A sweeping effort to "dry up" Key West occurred on February 17, 1926, when federal Prohibition agents from Miami raided approximately twenty-five bootlegging establishments and speakeasies around the city. This was the first Prohibition raid of any kind in Key West since 1924. Among the places raided were six within two blocks of the city's police station; one was across the street from the La Concha Hotel (one of the finest establishments in the city), and one was on Stock Island. Sheriff Roland Curry reported that fifteen people were arrested and placed in his jail. After the raids, customs service and U.S. Coast Guard personnel patrolled the streets of Key West all night to prevent rumrunners from unloading illicit cargo. However, a liquor dealer put the word out the next day that he had successfully stocked his warehouse under the noses of the authorities.

Miami

Miami was sometimes called the "Wild West" of Prohibition. Miami historian Paul George said, "South Florida probably flouted Prohibition more than any other part of the country." George also said, "There were speakeasies all up and down Flagler Street, where you'd tap on the door and utter the password to get inside. There were cars driving around with liquor in their rumble seats. Bordellos and gambling and booze. A red light district on Biscayne Bay between Northeast 13th Street and 16th Street." Perhaps one of the most telling facts about the influence that Prohibition had on the Miami area is that Dade County's population tripled from 34,000 to

102,000 residents from 1920 to 1925. The financial boom from illicit liquor certainly played a factor, as many people relocated to the area to capitalize on the potential for pocketing easy cash.

In a May 17, 1922 *Miami News* article titled "Washington Man Discovers a War Among Bootleggers; Miami Is Seat of Conflict," it was reported that bootleggers in the Miami area were "tipping off" the operations of their competitors. This led to many arrests and jail sentences. It seems that greed trumped the code of "honor among thieves."

B.W. Andrews, head of the legal division of the Prohibition unit, reported to Prohibition commissioner Hayes in Washington, D.C., that smuggling had been reduced more than 50 percent in the Miami area due to the bootleggers' war. This was obviously wishful thinking, as the volume of bootlegging in the Miami area increased after 1922.

Bands of hijackers worked together in the Miami area to rob bootleggers. This can be described as a game of crook robbing crook. Deputy Sheriff Earl Venno identified the hijacker groups as the Miami Avenue, the River, East Flagler, NW Twenty-Second Avenue and Fort Lauderdale. They had an unwritten agreement where the bands of hijackers would attack any well-protected liquor cache that did not have ties to any of these gangs.

An October 7, 1931 article in the *Miami Times* titled "Five Hi-Jacker Bands Operate—Liquor Pirates Divide Miami Area into Districts for Mutual Benefit" explains how this criminal network operated. The operation was particularly effective, as the article explains:

> *Hijackers are favored by law which declares liquor of no legal value, hence it cannot be stolen. Practically the only manner in which a hijacker could be held for trial is for a deputy sheriff or police officer to catch a hijacker in the act of holding up a bootlegger with a pistol. Then a charge of highway robbery or aggravated assault could be placed against him. But it is extremely unlikely that any bootlegger would testify against the hijacker because of fear of reprisals by his gangs.*

This profitable hijacking was very dangerous, as vicious street justice often intervened and took the law into their own hands. Rival crime syndicates sometimes severely beat hijackers and chased them out of town with a death threat if they ever returned. John B. Rowland, special investigator for the Florida state attorney's office, reported that two hijackers, George Edwards and Ortho D. Kennedy, were gunned down after a raid on a bootlegger's cache.

If a bootlegger signed an affidavit against a hijacker charging theft of liquor, it was possible that the bootlegger, a criminal in the eyes of the law, could be prosecuted. Two Miami bootleggers learned a hard lesson when they were prosecuted and convicted on the strength of their own affidavits. Both were sent to the federal penitentiary in Atlanta to do time for their violation of Prohibition laws.

Orlando

Orange County and the city of Orlando were no strangers to the prohibition of liquor. The county voted itself dry in 1907, so by the time national Prohibition became the law of the land, liquor had been banned for thirteen years in the area.

Orlando had many small bootlegging and moonshine operations that kept the liquor flowing around town. In the city, some moonshiners hid stills under the floorboards of their homes. In the wooded areas, larger moonshine stills, some with a one-hundred-gallon capacity, were camouflaged under trees and behind thickets.

Orlando had some speakeasies, some hidden in plain sight, that offered a night out on the town that included gambling, dancing, dining and illicit alcoholic beverages.

Some of Orlando's many soft drink parlors—nineteen were listed in the city directory in 1924—served as fronts for speakeasies. Perhaps the most well-known was the Pine Street Cold Drink Stand. Another soft drink parlor that was a front for a speakeasy was the Orange Drop located on Cheney Highway (now Colonial Drive). It was located outside the city limits of Orlando, which made it out of reach of the jurisdiction of the city's police department. In 1926, the Orange Drop was repurposed from a soda fountain to a nightclub. The owner, Sam Warren, rarely had issues with local authorities but did endure a couple of Prohibition raids by federal agents.

In 1929, the Orange Drop was upgraded with improvements and additions and reopened as the Flamingo Café. It became one of the area's well-known speakeasies and included Spanish cuisine, a dance floor, live entertainment, a gambling room and a bar serving a variety of illicit liquor. Reportedly, the Flamingo Café was frequented by Orlando's mayor and other public officials. Within a month of its grand opening, federal Prohibition agents raided the club and arrested Sam Warren, his business partner and two

The Flamingo Café was Central Florida's largest and best-equipped nightclub and served as a speakeasy during Prohibition. It was demolished in the late 1950s. *Courtesy of State Archives of Florida.*

waiters and seized around nine quarts of illicit liquor. The Flamingo Café opened the next day, but two months later, it was ordered closed by a judge. After nearly a year of being shuttered, the Flamingo Café opened again in January 1931. It suffered additional Prohibition raids but managed to stay in business past the repeal of Prohibition.

Palm Beach/West Palm Beach

Residents and visitors in Palm Beach and West Palm Beach skirted national Prohibition laws, similar to most areas in Florida, and found ways to keep liquor flowing. The Breakers (the historic Renaissance Revival–style luxury hotel) in Palm Beach had secret dining rooms built so guests could drink illicit alcoholic beverages discreetly. The Royal Poinciana Hotel (the Gilded Age luxury hotel) in Palm Beach included an illicit alcohol-serving bar that was accessed through a covert hallway called "Hypocrite's Row."

Almost all of the large estates in the area that were built during the 1920s had out-of-sight rooms designed to hide illicit alcoholic beverages. Existing estates remodeled rooms to secretly store illicit liquor. Joseph P. Kennedy Sr., father of President John F. Kennedy, had a hidden room behind his bar to store illicit alcohol in his Palm Beach estate.

The Mediterranean Revival house known as Palmeiral, located at 801 South County Road, had several features for bootlegging operations. It included a tunnel, around two hundred feet long, from the dunes to a twenty-by-thirty-foot basement storage room. Crawl spaces provided access from the basement storage room to a large walk-in refrigerator under the main kitchen and to a few bedrooms. There was also a secret storage room in the pool house that was accessed through underground crawl spaces.

In June 1921, Deputy Sheriff Stanley J. Wakely seized the largest professionally designed moonshine copper still ever seen in the area. The still had a fifty-gallon-per-day capacity. Also seized were fifteen barrels of mash, thirty-one empty fifty-gallon barrels and a large number of empty bottles. This still operation was believed to be the supplier of the highest-quality moonshine ever produced in the area.

Pensacola

During Prohibition, Pensacola had a few areas that were notorious for speakeasies and bootlegging. Sanders Beach and the waterfront neighborhood now known as Hawkshaw were locations well known for easy-flowing illicit liquor.

Arguably, the most notorious area of Pensacola during Prohibition was known as Luke's Alley. There were several homicides, Prohibition raids, illegal street gambling, speakeasies and other deviant acts of lawlessness prevalent around the area. Luke's Alley survived through the repeal of Prohibition; however, all of the surrounding buildings met the wrecking ball around 1940.

Dry agents and Deputy Marshal S.A. Johnson staged a dangerous all-night vigil to arrest four bootleggers operating a large still operation near Pensacola. Four bootleggers were using a tent for a hideout near the still. After the first two bootleggers were arrested, a car pulled up near the tent with two other bootleggers. A .32-caliber Smith and Wesson pistol was seized from the car after the initial arrest.

The dry agents destroyed the large 900-gallon capacity still and 61 gallons of mash whiskey. A second 150-gallon capacity still believed to be part of this operation was discovered in Jones swamp, about eight miles from Pensacola, and it was also destroyed by dry agents. A shootout was avoided, and all four men were held for federal court under $500 bonds.

Moonshine and liquor were not the only illicit alcoholic beverages federal agents were after during Prohibition. Home-brewers of beer also faced arrest if caught in the act, as a June 3, 1928 article in the *Pensacola News Journal* titled "Beer Raiders Launch Their Summer Drive" describes:

> *The summer beer-raiding season was opened yesterday by Pensacola Prohibition agents and the supply of foaming home brew was depleted.*
>
> *Federal officers made five arrests of alleged home brew dealers and seized 900 bottles of the product in addition to capping machines, crocks, bottles, caps, and other equipment.*
>
> *The agents made their largest haul in West Pensacola. Mrs. Charlotte Rech, residing six miles from Pensacola on the Nunez Ferry Highway, was found with 384 bottles of home brew on her premises, along with two 10-gallon crocks of fermented beer, 10 gallons of wine, and one pint of moonshine. She was released on a $300 bond.*
>
> *John Kirk, living in the vicinity of Kupfrain Park, north of the city, had 300 bottles of beer on his premises as well as 10 gallons of wine and a 10-gallon crock of fermented beer. He was lodged in the county jail and will be arraigned for bond Monday.*

Tampa

Tampa was one of the wettest spots in the United States during Prohibition due to three major sources of illicit liquor: smugglers operating from foreign countries, including the Bahamas, Cuba and Jamaica; local moonshiners; and local and statewide bootleggers. The geographical location of Tampa coupled with its numerous inlets and coves made it a haven for rumrunners. Large moonshining operations, some growing into commercial-style enterprises, arose in the vast rural areas around Hillsborough County. One of the more interesting characters of all the Tampa-area bootleggers was William Flynn. He was a cooper (wooden barrel craftsman) prior to Prohibition but soon afterward built an impressive three-still operation that was supplying much of the west side of Tampa. Flynn's luck ran out in the early days of Prohibition. On October 14, 1920, federal agents raided Flynn's still operation, arrested him and destroyed all of his equipment. Flynn was forced out of the bootlegging business, but other local moonshiners moved in and quickly supplied his customers.

Prohibition brought economic opportunities to many Italian immigrants living in the Tampa area as they became bootleggers. The illicit trade employed as many as 50 percent of Ybor City's families. Prohibition indoctrinated many Italian Americans into Tampa's criminal underworld, which was previously dominated by Cubans and Spaniards.

Many Tampa-area residents did not respect Prohibition laws and were actively involved in various smuggling and bootlegging activities. Corrupt city and county officials took bribes from the underworld and tipped criminals off to Prohibition raids. Most people arrested by local police for violation of Prohibition laws were given token fines by municipal judges and were back in business quickly, sometimes the same day. A Tampa-area law enforcement officer said, "Bootleggers made no bones of their business, smiled when arrested, paid up immediately, and continued to defy authorities."

When the area prohibitionists raised concerns about the well-known Tampa and Ybor City speakeasies and other alcohol-serving outlets (there were reportedly 130 different retailers selling illicit liquor in 1930), local police conducted raids, which led to temporary closings of speakeasies and coffeehouses. After the press reported these raids, the establishments quickly opened again.

A moonshine still and its accessories discovered in a house attic in Tampa, Florida, circa 1925. *Courtesy of State Archives of Florida.*

Occasionally, there were staged Prohibition raids where speakeasies and liquor dealers were forewarned by corrupt officials. All of the high-quality liquor was hidden, leaving only cheap moonshine to be confiscated by dry agents and local police. Those arrested were usually acquitted or given small fines and quickly returned to their illicit businesses.

To the surprise of Deputy Marshal J.E. Cox and revenue agent Jackson Gray, a large moonshine still was discovered in the heart of the city at 413 Twiggs Alley, near the Tampa Union Train Station. The still was poorly, and dangerously, constructed using a ten-foot gas pipe for a coil, a soap box for a stand and a lard can for a kettle. Forty-seven gallons of sour mash were seized and then poured out, and a keg of moonshine was discovered buried in a nearby chicken coop. The home's owner, Ned Jefferson, claimed friends were using his house and he did not know anything about the illicit still. Jefferson's denial was not taken seriously, as he was arrested and held on $300 bond.

A June 27, 1927 *Tampa Times* article describes a very unusual moonshining incident: "A regular old time 'meller-dramer' was enacted earlier yesterday morning at a frame house located at 1621-½ Fifth Avenue, when a moonshiner blew up his still just in time to escape arrest at the hands of 'them revenuers.'" After a man spotted undercover law enforcement officers watching his house, a large explosion soon shook the house, and debris from the roof, windows and walls was strewn all over the neighborhood. After the fire department extinguished the flames, a large still in the back room of the house was discovered to have been blown up. Fortunately, there were no injuries, but the house suffered extensive damage. A seventeen-year-old boy was identified as the moonshiner and the arsonist. He was arrested and charged with possession of a still and arson.

Smell of Moonshine Cannot Warrant a Raid in Florida

In 1932, a federal Prohibition agent said he "did smell the odor of fermenting mash emanating from the garage" south of the Palm Beach canal and east of Military Trail. Federal Prohibition agents then raided the property and discovered an operational moonshine still tucked away in a garage. James C. Weight and Ernest Fuchs were arrested and charged for violating Prohibition laws.

When the case came before Judge Halsted L. Ritter in the United States District Court, he ruled that "the smell of mash alone is not probable cause strong enough to give Prohibition agents the legal authority to raid a still." All charges against Weight and Fuchs were dropped.

NASCAR Roots Began with Bootlegging during Prohibition

A bootlegging strategy emerged during Prohibition when the engines in cars carrying illicit liquor were modified for greater speed so they could outrun police cars. Other modifications included the removal of floorboards and passenger and back seats (providing added space for illicit liquor), suspension strengthening and a protective radiator plate. Some of these modifications evolved into the sport of stock car racing, and as a result, the National Association for Stock Car Auto Racing (NASCAR) can trace its roots to the bootleggers of the Prohibition era.

Traveling during the Prohibition era required excellent driver skills, as many of the roads, especially in Florida, were dirt, gravel and single-lane backroads. Drivers often had to maneuver these rough roads after dark with no headlights.

In 1932, Ford Motor Company introduced the powerful V8 engine, and many police departments purchased these cars to combat the modified cars being used by bootleggers. Good mechanics were now in demand by bootleggers, and new modifications were required to outpace V8-powered police cars.

As bootleggers drove their cars at reckless speeds over dangerous roads, it was important to have the best available tires to withstand the strain. Several companies designed tires based on the requirements of the bootlegging trade.

In 1936, the city of Daytona Beach held the first organized stock car race as a promotion. Bill France, a Prohibition-era mechanic, placed fifth in this race; however, he was determined to develop an organized sport for stock car racing.

On December 14, 1947, France met with racers and promoters to discuss the creation of an official stock car racing sport. NASCAR was formed on February 21, 1948, in the Streamline Hotel's Ebony Bar in Daytona Beach. Many of NASCAR's early drivers and mechanics were former bootleggers during and after the Prohibition era.

Chapter 7

SELECTIVE AND UNEQUAL JUSTICE IN FLORIDA

During Prohibition, federal law enforcement in Florida concentrated on bootleggers, rumrunners and moonshiners but disproportionately targeted lawbreakers who were economically and socially disadvantaged. Many immigrants, Black, poor and working-class people were arrested for violations of Prohibition laws.

Public support for Prohibition was dwindling by the late 1920s, and many agents of the Bureau of Prohibition knew that its repeal would mean the end of their careers. As a result, they accelerated arrests for violations of Prohibition laws in an attempt to prove to the press, and the public, that these lawbreakers were still a major threat to society. Many of these arrests were petty moonshiners and bootleggers with little to no resources to challenge the legal system. These large numbers of arrests looked impressive on paper but did little to combat the major racketeers and crime syndicates who were producing, transporting and smuggling most of the illicit alcohol in Florida.

Many federal agents believed they lacked the resources, and at times did not have the motivation, to pursue the powerful crime syndicates who possessed money, heavily armed gangsters and expensive lawyers to fight legal battles.

Florida's Federal Courts Overwhelmed

In the final years of Prohibition, cases involving violations of Prohibition laws declined in Florida's lower and supreme courts due to revenue problems around the state. A debt crisis in Florida's counties and cities grew from $100 million in 1922 to $600 million in 1929. As a result, most local jurisdictions passed a large quantity of court cases and responsibility of Prohibition law enforcement on to the federal government. As an example, from 1929 to 1933, the Hernando County Circuit Court did not convict one person for violations of Prohibition laws.

As of August 4, 1927, there were 2,809 federal cases pending in the Southern District of Florida. As the number of violations of Prohibition laws kept flooding and bogging down the Florida courts, it appeared to many that an additional federal judge was required to assist with the overload of cases. As a comparison, in 1921 the Southern District of Florida settled 551 criminal prosecutions, which included 463 federal violations of Prohibition laws. The Northern District of Florida settled 164 criminal prosecutions, which included 121 federal violations of Prohibition laws.

In 1928, Senator Duncan U. Fletcher introduced a bill to add a third federal judge to the Southern District of Florida. On March 23, 1928, U.S. Supreme Court chief justice William H. Taft approved the proposal after realizing that the Southern District of Florida stretched for 520 miles and was a "convenient hiding and landing place for smugglers and rum runners."

In 1928, the Southern District of Florida settled 1,319 criminal prosecutions, which included 1,121 federal violations of Prohibition laws.

MOONSHINING INCREASES DURING GREAT DEPRESSION

On October 24, 1929, the Wall Street stock market crashed and initiated the Great Depression, which was the longest and most widespread economic crisis of the twentieth century. As a result, the unemployment rate in Florida rose, partially due to the decline of the tourist industry, which fell from three million to one million visitors per year. To make conditions worse, the Mediterranean fruit fly invaded the state and ruined about 60 percent of the citrus industry. Starting in 1929, the per capita income in Florida declined from $510 to $478 per year. In 1930, it fell to $392.35 per year. Over ninety thousand Florida families were in dire economic condition due to the Great Depression.

Many desperate people, most normally law abiding, turned to moonshining in an attempt to supplement their meager incomes. Many small-time moonshiners who typically had no community support or knowledge of the legal system were targeted and arrested by federal Prohibition agents.

Federal Prohibition agents knew if they arrested this class of people, they had a high probability of closing the case with a conviction.

An October 20, 1929 article in the *Pensacola News Journal* titled "Officers Drying Up This Area" discusses how federal and state officers conducted a series of raids over a period of a month in what was referred to as a "clean-up" in west Florida:

> *The past four weeks brought big results in Prohibition enforcement not only in Escambia County, but in all of west Florida, a check-up yesterday showed.*
>
> *Local federal officials and county authorities confiscated large quantities of moonshine and imported whiskies, destroyed moonshine distilling outfits by the dozens and confiscated several automobiles used in transporting liquors.*
>
> *Thirty-eight persons have been arrested and five automobiles confiscated by federal and county authorities.*
>
> *Six automobiles and imported liquors with an estimated retail value of $8,000 have been confiscated by customs border patrol officers who began operations in west Florida about a month ago.*
>
> *About 125 moonshine distilling outfits, 220 gallons of moonshine whiskey and 108 cases of imported liquors have been destroyed or confiscated by federal and county authorities.*
>
> *Local Prohibition agents made 21 arrests in west Florida and 12 of them in Holmes, Washington, and Walton counties in a single clean-up.*
>
> *They also confiscated or destroyed more than a dozen stills and confiscated or destroyed 155 gallons of moonshine and almost 100 barrels of mash of 50 gallons capacity each.*
>
> *County officers destroyed almost 100 moonshine distilling outfits with large quantities of beer and mash, 220 gallons of whiskey and made nine arrests.*

This article also demonstrates that local authorities did cooperate and work with federal law enforcement. Local law enforcement supplied leads to federal Prohibition agents regarding illicit moonshining and bootlegging and did occasionally testify in federal court.

"Commercial Violators"

After Prohibition's first ten years, the trials and tribulations of its enforcement led to better selection criteria and training, especially in legal schooling, of federal agents. As a result, better and stronger cases against violators of Prohibition laws were being handed over to federal district attorneys. The Bureau of Prohibition began concentrating on what it referred to as "commercial violators." The idea was to arrest the large operations instead of the numerous small private violators of Prohibition laws.

On December 8, 1932, Amos W.W. Woodcock, director of the Bureau of Prohibition, said:

> *This objective seems correct, both tactically and strategically—tactically because commercial violators have many constitutional and statutory protections—strategically because the commercial violator is the source from*

Officers Locate Big Moonshine Factory

Part of a gigantic distillery near Thonotosassa raided by Hillsborough officers the other day. It was capable of filling a five-gallon jug with shine every 15 minutes. Authorities said that it was the production plant for a syndicate of Tampa liquor men. —Photo by Cole.

"Officers Locate Big Moonshine Factory." *From the* Tampa Times, *April 26, 1930.*

which most private violations originate and because commercial violators are the kind of offenders which our people expect the law to reach.

The Bureau of Prohibition was obviously connecting commercial violators with organized crime syndicates who had vast resources and financial backing, which mostly enabled them to stay one step ahead of the law. In reality, federal agents were equating commercial violators to any person, mostly small-time moonshiners and bootleggers. Some arrests by federal agents were for possessing moonshine in amounts as small as one pint.

Unequal Racial Justice in Florida

The Jim Crow era (1877–1968) was characterized by a historical racial divide in the United States, specifically in the Deep South, which included Florida. During the years of Prohibition, Jim Crow laws were enforced in Florida. Jim Crow laws legally enforced the segregation of facilities, services and education in society by racial groups (mainly Blacks or "colored" and Whites). All non-Whites were considered "colored."

Most opportunities for Black people in education, employment and elsewhere were limited. During the Jim Crow era, White people held most of the political offices and owned most of the businesses in Florida. Most Black people were employed in low-paying and labor-intensive jobs.

The *Plessy v. Ferguson*, 163 U.S. 537 case in 1896 was a landmark U.S. Supreme Court decision that actually upheld the constitutionality of racial segregation. This high court decision established the doctrine of "separate but equal." However, there was never any equality among the races during the Jim Crow era.

The selective nature of federal law enforcement sometimes focused on the racial tensions in Florida. Black people were oftentimes singled out as easy targets, as they typically had little money to challenge the White-dominated legal system and were often given longer jail sentences if convicted.

Prohibition actually created opportunities for Black men and women to make extra money working on rumrunning vessels, bootlegging and moonshining. Of course, these were illegal activities that could lead to arrests, fines, prison sentences and even death.

Following are some stories that demonstrate how active some Black men and women were in illicit alcohol trades during Prohibition. During the

Jim Crow era, the mainstream press oftentimes referred to Black men as "negroes" and Black women as "negresses" and often exaggerated some of their alcohol offenses as well.

King of the Negro Bootleggers

A June 19, 1926 article in the *Orlando Sentinel* titled "Raid on Negro's Home Nets Twelve Gallons of Liquor" describes a raid by Sheriff Karel and Deputies Dority, McDowell, Peel and Caruthers. Arrested was T. Dennis, whom law enforcement referred to as the "King of Negro Bootleggers." The law enforcement officers discovered twelve gallons of liquor hidden in an attic behind a false trapdoor. Dennis was arrested for possessing intoxicating liquor and then released on a $500 bond pending appearance in a criminal court.

On July 16, 1926, Dennis was arrested again for possessing intoxicating liquor, this time only one gallon. Police reported that he was a well-known bootlegger who had been arrested multiple other times.

On July 17, 1928, Dennis was sentenced to sixty days in the Orange County Jail and ordered to pay a $150 fine.

The truth was that T. Dennis was a small-time bootlegger who was targeted and arrested multiple times for possessing relatively small quantities of moonshine. Yet law enforcement in the Orlando area referred to him as the "King of Negro Bootleggers."

Queen of Negro Bootleggers

A December 25, 1921 article in the *Tampa Bay Times* titled "Queen of Negro Bootleggers Is Re-Arrested" stated an arrest made by Deputy Sheriffs Charles Simms and James Hance was that of Mattie Johnson, "Queen of Negro Bootleggers." She was placed in the county jail under a $200 bond and held for a court appearance on a charge of possessing illicit moonshine. Johnson had only a small amount of liquor in her possession, yet law enforcement in the Tampa Bay area referred to her as the "Queen of Negro Bootleggers."

First Small Liquor Possession Offense: Big Fine or Ninety Days in Jail

A July 2, 1931 article in the *News Press* titled "Liquor Possession Cause of Big Fine" highlights how a Black woman's first liquor possession offense could have landed her in jail: "Lillian Rutledge, negress, was fined $60 and costs or sentenced to 90 days in jail [by County Judge L.Y. Redwine] after pleading guilty to charges of the possession and sale of liquor in county court."

She was arrested by Officer Charlie Brown of the Safety Hill Police Department and Deputy Sheriffs Roy Larson and C.L. McMillan in a cabaret she operated along with her husband. Her husband was released after Lillian disclosed that the illicit liquor was her property.

KKK Raids and Kidnaps Black Moonshiners

A May 8, 1924 article in the *Tampa Tribune* titled "White Robed Figures Raid Negro Shiners" highlights how members of the KKK raided several Black-owned businesses and kidnapped their proprietors: "15 white-robed figures are said to have entered three negro cabarets in the colored section known as Jacksonville, removed the alleged proprietors, namely, Joe Weightmen, Randolph Coleman, and one Williams and departed with them for parts unknown."

The article also stated, "While the reputed saloons of Jacksonville were being raided…Officers Ott, Daughety, with an assistant, conducted a search of a house in Tato' Quarters, between Cleveland and Drew streets, and captured half a gallon of moonshine liquor and one negro named More, while another darkey in the same room escaped. A practical campaign against bootleggers appears to be on in Clearwater."

Chapter 8

TRAGIC PROHIBITION-RELATED DEATHS IN FLORIDA

One of the unforeseen consequences of Prohibition was the number of tragic deaths it caused to innocent bystanders, normal citizens, law enforcement personnel and lawbreakers. Many people were killed by criminals pursing the profits of illicit liquor. Others were killed in armed encounters with federal agents, state police and local law enforcement agencies.

A February 27, 1924 article in the *Tampa Tribune* titled "Booze Deaths" reported, "The bootleggers' death toll for 1923, officially reported, may pass 2,500 as compared with 1,611 deaths in 1922." The article also callously stated, "At that the death list is a small one compared to the number of men who drank themselves to death in the saloon days when the nation spent $2,500,000,000 yearly for drink."

Following are some of the tragic Prohibition-related deaths that occurred in Florida.

Federal Agents, Sheriffs and Deputies Killed

Explosion Kills St. Lucie County Sheriff "W.R." Monroe

On March 26, 1921, tragedy struck the St. Lucie County Sheriff's Department when Sheriff W.R. Monroe was killed in a boat explosion. Earlier that day, Sheriff Monroe and Deputy Sheriff Donaldson had seized a boat loaded with illicit liquor and were sailing it back to dock on the Indian River. Onboard the boat at the time of the explosion were Sheriff Monroe, Deputy Sheriff Donaldson and Dozier Drawdy, alleged rumrunner. The explosion threw all three men overboard. Donaldson and Drawdy were able to swim to safety, but Sheriff Monroe was fatally injured. Donaldson said he was slightly burned, but his survival was an almost miraculous escape from death.

Federal Prohibition Officer W.H. Schreck issued warrants for the arrest of the two rumrunners, Terrell Hayes and D. Drawdy, who were operating the rumrunning boat that later exploded. They were charged with violation of Prohibition laws.

The Deadly Pasco County Ambush

On October 4, 1922, Constable Arthur Crenshaw of the Pasco County Sheriff's Office and federal Prohibition agent John Van Waters were shot dead in an ambush in Pasco County while investigating illegal still operations. As Crenshaw and Waters were sitting in a car, a barrage of gunfire erupted, killing both of them. Six men were arrested, five of them brothers, and charged with two counts of murder. During their trial, all six were found not guilty of the murder charge.

On February 24, 1925, one of these men was killed in a Prohibition raid near the same spot where Agent Waters and Constable Crenshaw were killed.

Dry Agent "Pistol Pete" Bowdoin Killed in Shootout

Federal Prohibition agent James Edmon "Pistol Pete" Bowdoin, circa 1924. *Courtesy of State Archives of Florida.*

On February 16, 1925, federal Prohibition agent James Edmon "Pistol Pete" Bowdoin and two deputies were tracking alleged bootleggers after being tipped that they were preparing to transport a large load of moonshine from a still operation located on a remote island. Bowdoin spotted three bootleggers (Bernie Harris, Harvey Walker and Sumpter Harris) while they were hauling a load of moonshine on a boat on Wright's Creek near Caryville, Washington County. Bowdoin was shot in the arm after being spotted by the bootleggers, and a shootout ensued where Bowdoin shot and killed Bernie Harris and Walker. Sumpter Harris suffered a broken thigh during the melee. The two deputies were scouting a potential boat landing area a mile away. When they arrived at the scene of the shootout, they found Bowdoin in his car dead from multiple gunshot wounds.

Agent James E. Bowdoin was a former deputy sheriff of Manatee County and one of Florida's most well-known and charismatic revenuers. He earned the nickname of "Pistol Pete" due to his proficient abilities with handguns.

A.L. Allen, Prohibition director from Tampa, personally directed federal Prohibition agents to search the area where the shootout occurred. The agents discovered a large one-hundred-gallon-capacity still and sixty gallons of mash whiskey on the island, which was almost impregnable due to thick undergrowth. Several other smaller still operations were discovered as well, proving the area was a mecca for moonshining.

Buchanan v. State *(Florida Supreme Court, 1928)*

In December 1926, J.W. Buchanan and D.W. Blue returned to Buchanan's cottage near Perry, Taylor County, from a hunting trip. Two men, Prohibition agents Jacob P. Brandt and Walter D. Mobray, pulled up in a car in front of Buchanan's cottage and sounded the car's horn. Buchanan invited the Prohibition agents inside his home. A short time later, both agents, Brandt and Mobray, were dead after being gunned down by Buchanan.

During Buchanan's initial murder trials (one for the murder of Brandt and the other for the murder of Mobray), he claimed that the agents unlawfully entered his home and he shot them in self-defense after they tried to shoot him. A local sheriff, his hunting partner D.W. Blue, and several of Buchanan's neighbors testified against him.

Government prosecutors claimed that the Prohibition agents knew Buchanan was making and selling moonshine and went to Buchanan's cottage to purchase some for evidence in order to obtain a search warrant. The prosecutors believe that Buchanan became hostile to the agents' plan and grabbed two guns from inside the house and opened fire. Mobray was hit by bullets and tried to escape but only managed to run twenty-five feet before collapsing to the ground dead. Brandt was shot in the shoulder with a pistol and then crawled under the cottage for protection, but Buchanan followed him and killed him with blasts from a shotgun.

In both trials, Buchanan was found guilty of murder. Claiming mistrial, Buchanan appealed to the Florida Supreme Court, which found the original trials to be accurate.

The abstract from *Buchanan v. State* discusses the evidence that helped to determine Buchanan's guilt:

> *The case consisted in many elements of circumstantial evidence, particularly in so far as the defendant's motives for killing the men were involved. The evidence tended to show his attitude toward all persons, including officers, who should come upon his place to search it for contraband liquors. The men who were killed had appeared at the defendant's house as officers of the law to search his premises for whiskey. They advised him of the fact. He knew their purpose. The evidence tended to show his mental attitude toward those men and in so far was contradictory of the theory that he killed in self-defense. There was no error in that ruling.*

Buchanan v. State was the Florida Supreme Court's first, and last, homicide case related to Prohibition enforcement. This case demonstrated that the local community and the Florida state courts did not obstruct the enforcement of federal Prohibition laws in this particular case. However, this was not always the story in Florida, as local and state law enforcement officials, politicians, the court system and community resistance often interfered with the enforcement of federal Prohibition laws.

Flagler County Sheriff Perry Hall Killed by a Bootlegger

On August 20, 1927, Flagler County sheriff Perry Edward Hall conducted a Prohibition raid in Roy, a rural, swampy, predominantly Black settlement in northeast Flagler County. Sheriff Hall entered a one-room shack with his pistol drawn and discovered several Black men inside with a cache of moonshine. Hall saw a suspected bootlegger, James Smith, pouring moonshine into a glass and ordered him to stand up. Smith suddenly smashed a whiskey bottle on Hall's head, which fractured his skull. Hall was taken to a hospital in St. Augustine but died several hours later.

One of the suspected bootleggers, Henry Williams, was arrested and held in the Flagler County Jail. He was placed under heavy guard for fear of vigilante mob violence.

Flagler County sheriff Perry Edward Hall, circa 1926. *Courtesy of the Flagler County Historical Society.*

The Florida Sheriff's Association offered a $100 reward and Florida governor John W. Martin offered $200 for the capture of James Smith. A Wild West–style posse was formed, assisted by Deputy A.P. Turlington of St. Johns County, and a frantic manhunt for James Smith ensued. The posse swarmed over a three-county area, and the manhunt quickly expanded south and north into Georgia.

Flagler County deputy sheriff George W. "Son" Durrance went to Greenland, Duval County, pursuing a lead and set up a stakeout near a water tower. Durrance was approached by a man whom he thought was the fugitive James Smith and ordered him to raise his hands. A shootout ensued where both men were shot; Durrance suffered a severe shotgun blast to his right side. It turned out that the other man, named Payne, was the night watchman at the local post office, and he thought Durrance was a robber. Deputy Sheriff Durrance died at age thirty-four, just three days after Sheriff Perry Hall was killed. According to the investigating officers, this incident was caused by an error in judgment by both men.

The largest Ku Klux Klan funeral ever known to have taken place in Flagler County, attended by several hundred Klansmen, was held for George W. Durrance on September 1, 1927, in the Espanola Cemetery. A September 1, 1927 *Flagler Tribune* article reported the event:

> *Several hundred Klansmen met the funeral cortege, which, it was said, was the longest ever seen in this territory. Inside the burying ground the Klansmen formed in ranks about the grave. Everything was still, the members of the Klan observed perfect silence, except when they sang. Afterwards the leader read the Klan ritual for the dead, which was most impressive. When the service was over, the galaxy of white-clad Klansmen dispersed as quickly as they had assembled, and within a few minutes none were to be seen.*

Three weeks after Sheriff Hall's murder, his assailant, James Smith, was tracked down in Georgia by a posse composed of the entire Tift County Sheriff's Department and some civilians. A September 12, 1927 *News Press* article titled "Florida Negro Shot in Georgia" describes what happened:

> *A negro believed to be George Jones alias Jim Smith wanted for the murder of Sheriff Perry Hall on August 20, was shot and killed near Brooksfield, it became known today. A sheriff's posse had surrounded the negro in a house, officers said, and the negro attempted to flee through the back door when he was shot down. The body will be taken back to Florida for positive identification.*

Florida governor John W. Martin appointed W.J. Williams, a deputy sheriff, as Flagler County sheriff to replace Perry Hall.

Two Dry Agents Gunned Down while Serving Warrant

On January 18, 1930, Robert K. Moneure and F.R. Patterson, dry agents, attempted to raid the West Palm Beach home of George W. Moore, alleged bootlegger, under the authority of a search warrant issued by a U.S. commissioner. The warrant was issued because dry agents were watching Moore's home and observed a truckload of liquor being delivered earlier in the day. After the warrant was issued, they also observed Moore receiving twelve quarts of liquor from an alleged bootlegger. Moore was well acquainted with dry agent Moneure, as he had assisted in a Prohibition raid at Moore's home the previous summer and seized 180 cases of illicit liquor.

When the dry agents approached Moore with the warrant, he shot and killed both of them. E.M. Baynes, attorney for Moore, stated, "They overstepped their bounds and the shooting followed…They made an attempt to break into Moore's home with a warrant that did not permit search after nightfall."

Moore was taken into custody and placed in the county jail pending charges. Robert E. Tuttle, Prohibition administrator, turned his evidence over to the Florida state courts and asked that Moore be charged for two counts of murder. Tuttle stated, "These officers lost their lives while performing their regular duties in serving a federal search warrant at the home of George Moore…This warrant was exhibited to Moore by Moneure with a request that Moore open the door and allow the search to proceed." Tuttle went on to report, "Moore ran into the house and slammed the door, whereupon Moneure gained admission to the porch…As Moneure reached the closed front door a shot was fired from the inside, tearing a hole through the door and taking effect in Moneure's forehead, causing instant death." Dry agent James Kugler was standing beside Moneure when he was shot. Dry agents

F.R. Patterson and James McNalty then entered the rear door of Moore's home. Moore charged toward them and shot and killed Patterson.

Bureau of Prohibition commissioner J.M. Doran issued a statement where he blamed the killing of Moneure and Patterson on "the recent inflammatory attacks upon our personnel." Doran also said he had "prohibited agents from using weapons except in defense of their lives or the lives of their comrades." He added, "The agents under these instructions would let a Prohibition violator escape rather than resort to the use of firearms."

This case gained widespread notoriety for its test of "sunset raids." The southern federal district court ruled that sunset was not the end of the day, and daytime search warrants could be executed after sunset if there was visible light. The court also ruled that nighttime is "the hour at which one could no longer see a person at a distance." Moore was found guilty of forcibly resisting a government officer and sentenced to ten years in a federal penitentiary.

Bootleggers and Moonshiners Killed

Federal Agents Kill Moonshiner in Cypress Swamp Shootout

On May 1, 1920, a shootout between an outfit of moonshiners and federal revenue agents, standing knee-deep in mud, took place in a cypress swamp near Tampa. Moonshiner Allen Ellis was killed, and his accomplice B.H. Love was seriously wounded in the melee.

It was reported that this outfit of moonshiners had sworn to kill the first revenuer who ventured into their swamp encampment. Their moonshine operation was hidden in a dense swamp surrounded by towering cypress trees and thick underbrush.

These threats did not deter federal revenue agents as they organized a raid. While the agents were sneaking up on the moonshine camp, one of the moonshiners grabbed a gun. Agent Williams shouted, "Throw up your hands!" The moonshiners, outnumbering the federal agents at least two to one, abruptly opened fire. An intense shootout with both rifles and pistols broke out, and dense smoke hung low over the water, blocking the view of all the combatants. The shootout continued until both sides spent all of their ammunition. As the smoke cleared, the federal agents were finally able to approach the camp and discovered that the moonshiners had retreated into the swamp. One dead and one wounded moonshiner were all that remained in the camp. The federal agents had to leave the wounded man at the camp as they went back to Tampa to notify an ambulance to respond to the scene.

When the still was analyzed, it was no mystery as to why so many criminals had risked their lives to protect it. "The distilling apparatus was an immense affair, the largest yet captured around here and said to have the capacity of 120 gallons every forty-eight hours. It was a double still, composed of two fifty-five gallon drums, with a first-class copper worm. There were seven barrels containing three or four hundred gallons of mash. There was also a large amount of cane syrup in gallon cans, reported to have been stolen. Some of the cans bore the name of O.P. Scally of Thonotosassa, who has recently lost a large amount of syrup by theft."

Law enforcement brought enough evidence back to their headquarters to be used in court and demolished the remaining still operation equipment and supplies.

Lynching and Decapitation: Moonshiner's "Death Code"

On December 31, 1923, the Duval County Sheriff's Department and the Jacksonville Police Department reported that two Black moonshiners were murdered. "Eugene Burman, negro, lynched Sunday afternoon near Jacksonville by a band of White men, and Edgar Phillips, negro, whose headless body was found in McGirt's Creek Saturday," were victims of a "death code" practiced by Duval County moonshiners. According to police, this death code includes capital punishment for various offenses committed in the illicit moonshining trade.

Duval County sheriff Deputy Frank Jones said, "Burman was working for moonshiners...I believe he was killed because he informed officials of the source of 25 gallons of moonshine whiskey found when he was arrested. If he did not give out information at least his slayers thought, he had."

Federal Prohibition agents had recently raided several moonshining operations in the outlying sections of Jacksonville. However, F.A. Hazeltine, divisional Prohibition chief, denied that Phillips and Burman were informers.

Moonshiners Using Sulfuric Acid Killed by Police

In October 1922, moonshiner W.A. Hudnell and his son Roy were killed in a shootout with county sheriffs and Tampa city police officers. The two moonshiners were attempting to deliver poisonous moonshine to what police referred to as the "negro section of town."

After the shootout, police went to the Hudnell residence to get a signature from Mrs. Hudnell to allow them to dispose of the automobile the moonshiners were using when they were killed. While at the Hudnell residence, the police made a very disturbing discovery: a moonshine operation that was actually using sulfuric acid as an additive. Sulfuric acid is very toxic and causes severe irritation of the nose and throat and is corrosive if inhaled or if it comes in contact with the skin or eyes. It can cause an accumulation of fluid in the lungs, which can be life-threatening. If ingested, it can cause permanent internal damage and even death.

In a barn on the Hudnell property were two forty-gallon-capacity moonshine stills, and nearby were two one-gallon bottles, partially used, and four empty bottles of sulfuric acid. Police destroyed the stills, thirty-two barrels of corn syrup mash and twelve gallons of moonshine.

During further investigation, Sheriff W.S. Lindsey discovered that W.A. Hudnell had been purchasing large quantities of sulfuric acid from a Clearwater druggist.

The death of these rogue moonshiners, W.A. Hudnell and his son Roy, and the destruction of their poisonous moonshine operation most likely prevented untold suffering and possibly the death of many people in the Tampa and Clearwater areas.

B.H. Roberson Killed and His Heart Partially Cut Out

In 1925, Mr. and Mrs. J.A. Conner were convicted of first-degree murder. Their victim was B.H. Roberson. The murder took place in Gilchrist County at a roadside filling station over the theft of a moonshine still.

"The records show that the couple, with their son, Hoyette Conner, met up with Roberson, and that Mrs. Conner cursed him and urged that Roberson's heart be cut out of his body, that she desired to 'boil it.' A fight followed, and the elder Conner was convicted of inflicting a deep [stabbing] wound in Roberson's side, one witness testified that he could really see that a portion of the dead man's heart had been cut off."

Mr. and Mrs. Conner were sent to the state penitentiary for life.

Murdered Bootlegger Discovered in Shack

On January 8, 1925, the body of Calvin A. Palmer, automobile mechanic and bootlegger, was discovered in a shack south of Miami with a gag stuffed in his mouth. Palmer was strangled and his skull fractured from being beaten on the head with an iron.

This murder was believed to be connected to two others: Joseph C. Boylan's body was discovered washed up on the beach with a severed jugular vein on December 28, 1924, and Warren G. Snowden's body was discovered on Miami Beach drowned with no evidence of salt water in his lungs.

Police believed that these murders stemmed from troubles between rival bootlegging gangs in the Miami area.

"Under-Cover" Man's Bullet-Riddled Body Found in River

A March 26, 1926 article in the *Tampa Tribune* titled "Bullet-Riddled Body of Negro Informer Is Found in River" describes how an undercover man working for the Tampa Police Department was brutally murdered.

> *The bullet-riddled body of Charles Ward, 50-year-old negro "under-cover" man for the police department, was found yesterday afternoon on the east side of the Hillsborough river, near the Tampa Terrace estates.*
>
> *Police are positive that negro bootleggers, emulating the gang warfare of New York and Chicago, shot Ward to death in revenge for tips on their activities that he furnished city detectives from time to time.*
>
> *The body was discovered by B.J. Mack, foreman of the J.E. Toney Construction Company. Five bullets had been fired into his body in the region of the heart. He had been dead for two to three days when found.*
>
> *A small metal tag on a string around his neck disclosed his connection with the police department. Ward has worked as an under-cover man for the police for some time. He has been instrumental in the conviction of a number of negro bootleggers and gamblers, and proved a valuable man in the solving of negro crimes, police said.*

Jacksonville's "King of the Bootleggers" Killed in Shootout

John Hysler was known as the "King of the Bootleggers" and the "Whiskey King of Duval County." He had many underworld connections, including Al Capone, and provided a source of income for many people in the Jacksonville area.

In September 1928, he was hauling a load of bootleg whiskey from Mineral City (present-day Ponte Vedra Beach) in his Chrysler roadster. He stopped at a toll booth on the St. Johns River Bridge (present-day Acosta Bridge). Two dry agents confronted him, and a shootout suddenly broke out. Hysler and dry agent Hope King both emptied their pistols at each other and were both severely injured during the bloody melee. J.E. Starratt, toll-taker, went to Hysler's car and asked if he needed help. Hysler said, "My god, he hit me all over. I'm full of lead." Later that night, Hysler died in a local hospital, and agent Hope was in critical condition.

Hysler's funeral drew more than 1,500 people, including many appreciative city residents and wealthy businessmen. Policeman, politicians and lawyers served as pallbearers, and one of the area's most respected clergymen performed the funeral services.

Rumrunners Killed

Mystery of the Wrecked British Schooner off Flagler Beach

In 1925, a British schooner carrying a large cargo of quality liquor wrecked off the coast of Flagler Beach. Law enforcement officials investigating the shipwreck found only one survivor onboard, the Black skipper. He refused to disclose his identity or the ownership of the vessel. Soon after being escorted ashore, he died. He was buried in an unmarked grave west of the Flagler Beach Coast Guard Station (present-day Gamble Rogers Memorial State Recreation Area). The mystery of who the Black rumrunning skipper was, the identity of the ship and the fates of the other crew members has never been solved.

"King of the Florida Smugglers" Gunned Down by Coast Guard

On February 24, 1926, E.W. "Red" Shannon (known as the "King of the Florida Smugglers" and "Miami's Bootleg King") was being pursued in his thirty-foot boat, *Goose*, in Biscayne Bay by a U.S. Coast Guard vessel. Shannon's boat slowed down as it was between two yachts, the *Rascal* and *Sunshine*, and had little opportunity of escape. The U.S. Coast Guard vessel pulled up, and a Coastie yelled to Shannon and his rumrunning accomplices, Addison Nickerson and Fred Walters, to put their hands in the air, as they believed the *Goose* might attempt to ram into their vessel. The *Goose* was near the exclusive Flamingo Hotel when the U.S. Coast Guard opened fire in plain sight of witnesses. Shannon was hit by a bullet, placed on a mattress on the hotel's lawn and then rushed to the Allison Hospital in Miami Beach. He died the next morning.

A February 27, 1926 *Miami Tribune* article describes what eyewitnesses were saying at a coroner's inquest into Shannon's death: "Vehemently denouncing the Miami Coast Guard personnel, voluntary witnesses at the inquest swore last night that 'Red' Shannon, Miami's 'bootleg king,' was shot from behind in cold blood Thursday night [February 24, 1926] as he stood with arms raised above his head in surrender." This article included the testimony of F.P. McGhan of the King Undertaking chapel, who said, "The rum king was shot in the back, near the base of the spine, the bullet coming out through his chest."

During the federal trial, several U.S. Coast Guard officers said that this case was the first time in the history of national customs laws that the U.S. Coast Guard's right to fire into a fleeing boat that was not heeding instructions was actually questioned.

On February 24, 1928, a federal jury in Miami found the five coast guardsmen (Ensign Philip Shaw, who was in charge, and four crewmen: Austin, McCaul, Meeking and Smith) not guilty of murder.

U.S. Coast Guard Executes the "Gulf Stream Pirate"

On August 7, 1926, a U.S. Coast Guard patrol boat was heading to Bimini to investigate alleged counterfeiting operations when the commander spotted a suspicious motorboat. The patrol boat fired across the bow of this motorboat and ordered it to stop. When the U.S. Coast Guard boarded the motorboat, they discovered illicit liquor, James Horace Alderman and Robert Weech.

James Horace Alderman, Prohibition-era smuggler who was executed by the U.S. Coast Guard, circa 1929. *Courtesy of Wikimedia Commons.*

Alderman had quite a reputation as a notorious South Florida rumrunner who used fast boats to outrun U.S. Coast Guard vessels and was widely known as the "Gulf Stream Pirate." The two men were arrested, and their cargo of liquor was brought onboard the U.S. Coast Guard patrol boat, which had a crew of seven Coasties and a Secret Service agent.

Alderman somehow obtained a handgun and started shooting. When the smoke cleared, Robert Webster, Secret Service agent, and Sidney C. Sanderlin, boatswain, were dead. Victor A. Lamby, motor machinist, was severely injured and later died. Jodie L. Hollingsworth, seaman second class, was shot in the eye; however, he survived. After the shootings, Alderman threatened to make the surviving U.S. Coast Guardsmen walk the gangplank, but the able men rushed him and held him prisoner.

At his federal murder trial, Alderman testified that he was abused, deprived of private rights and had his life threatened. He claimed these reasons were justification for killing the three men. Rumrunner Robert Weech testified against Alderman and received a light sentence of a year and a day in prison.

Alderman was found guilty of murdering Sidney C. Sanderland and Victor A. Lamby. At an earlier trial, Alderman was found guilty of murdering Robert Webster. On January 27, 1928, Judge Henry D. Clayton sentenced Alderman to death by hanging. His execution was scheduled for May 11, 1928, at the Broward County Jail in Fort Lauderdale. This was the first time in United States history that a death by hanging sentence was given to a rumrunner for murder on the high seas.

As Alderman sat in the county jail awaiting his execution, he reportedly found religion and then wrote an autobiography titled *The Life Story of James Horace Alderman.*

Hundreds of residents in South Florida signed a petition for clemency by recommending that Alderman's sentence be commuted from death to life in prison. Judge Henry D. Clayton and eleven members of the jury also petitioned for clemency for Alderman. Higher courts, including the U.S. Supreme Court, rejected clemency for Alderman, as did President Herbert Hoover.

The Broward County commissioners insisted that the hanging should be conducted on U.S. property. The U.S. Coast Guard decided to hang Alderman in a metal hangar at Coast Guard Base Six near Fort Lauderdale. A wood gallows structure was built inside the metal hangar specifically for Alderman's hanging.

On August 17, 1929, Alderman was hanged at Coast Guard Base Six. This was the only hanging ever conducted by the U.S. Coast Guard and the only legal hanging in Broward County history.

U.S. Coast Guard Threatened

On August 26, 1927, an anonymous letter was sent to U.S. Coast Guard commander Beckwith Jordan at Fort Lauderdale's Base Six. The letter stated:

> *You may think it all right to murder men, but this is to notify you and all others interested that for each man you kill the lives of three Prohibition grafters will be knocked off.*
>
> *A condition has been created by fanatics and self-appointed reformers that you and others think gives you the right to murder. It is due time that your mind should be disabused of this idea. Dealing in whiskey is legitimate. The 18th Amendment does not change that fact. There are enough grafters and fanatics in this country to ram it down our throats.*
>
> *Play this on your piano.*

The U.S. Coast Guard investigated the incident and attempted to locate the source of the letter. Investigators assumed it originated from associates of James Horace Alderman.

The Ashley Gang

One of the most notorious criminal gangs in all of Florida during the 1910s and 1920s was the Ashley Gang. The patriarch of the gang was John Hopkin Ashley, an incorrigible outlaw, bank robber, bootlegger and rumrunning pirate. He was sometimes referred to as the "King of the Everglades" or the "Swamp Bandit." He was a folk hero to many poor "Florida crackers" because of his anti-establishment stance against law enforcement, banks, politicians and wealthy landowners.

In 1912, John Ashley was suspected in the murder of DeSoto Tiger, a Seminole trapper and son of Tommy Tiger, chieftain of the Cow Creek Seminoles. When DeSoto Tiger's body was discovered, it was revealed that he had been shot in the back. He was last seen alive with John Ashley. After Ashley surrendered, he was held in the Palm Beach Jail awaiting trial for murder. He managed to escape from the jailhouse and fled into the Florida Everglades.

The Ashley Gang was formed and operated from different hideouts within the rough terrain and swamps of the Everglades. John became the leader of the Ashley Gang. Its other members were Joe, his father; Bob, Ed and Frank, his brothers; Hanford Mobley, his nephew; and a seasoned Chicago bank robber named "Kid" Lowe.

Between 1915 and 1924, the Ashley Gang robbed at least forty banks, netting nearly $1 million. During a 1915 bank robbery in Stuart, the Ashley Gang got into a shootout during their getaway, and a bullet fired by Kid Lowe bounced off the rear window frame of a car and shattered John's jaw, which blinded his right eye. A posse hunted John down and captured him in the Everglades. He was transported to Miami to stand trial for the murder of DeSoto Tiger. He was fitted with a glass eye while in prison.

On June 2, 1915, John Ashley's brother Bob attempted to break him out of the Dade County Jail. Bob knocked on the door of Deputy Sheriff Wilber W. Hendrickson's residence, which was adjacent to the Dade County Jail, and shot and killed him as he opened his door. He grabbed the jailhouse keys from Deputy Hendrickson's body but dropped them when he saw Hendrickson's wife holding a rifle. Bob ran away from Hendrickson's house and hijacked a delivery truck. Miami police officer John Rhinehart "Bob" Riblet caught up with Bob Ashley, and they engaged in a shootout. Both Officer Riblet and Bob Ashley were killed during the melee. Officer Riblet became the first Miami police officer killed in the line of duty, which shocked the community.

The following day, John Ashley's lawyer was able to convince State of Florida prosecutors to drop the murder change of DeSoto Tiger in exchange for Ashley's agreement to be peacefully moved to West Palm Beach and stand trial for the Stuart bank robbery. John Ashley pleaded guilty and was sentenced to seventeen and a half years in the state penitentiary at Raiford.

In March 1918, John Ashley escaped from the Raiford State Penitentiary and rejoined the Ashley Gang in the Everglades.

When Prohibition became the law of the land in 1920, the Ashley Gang capitalized on bootlegging and the operation of moonshine stills in Palm

Beach County. John, Ed and Frank Ashley operated rumrunning routes from the Bahamas into Jupiter Inlet and Stuart.

In 1920, John met and fell in love with .38-caliber pistol-packing Laura Beatrice Upthegrove, who gained the nickname "Queen of the Everglades." She cased banks to rob and was a lookout for the gang's still operations and hideouts in the Everglades.

In 1921, John was arrested in Wauchula while bootlegging liquor. He was sent back to the Raiford State Penitentiary. His brothers Ed and Frank disappeared in the Atlantic Ocean while on a rumrunning trip to Bimini. They were never heard of or seen again.

The Ashley Gang was now operating with Clarence Middleton, Hanford Mobley, Laura Upthegrove, Joe Ashley, Joe Tracy, Ray "Shorty" Lynn and Roy "Young" Mathews. They were known to rumrunners as ruthless pirates who would hijack illicit liquor cargos on the high seas.

On May 12, 1922, the Ashley Gang robbed the Bank of Stuart, the same bank it had robbed in 1915.

In September 1923, John Ashley was able to escape from Raiford State Penitentiary again. He rejoined the Ashley Gang, and they robbed many banks in South Florida.

On January 9, 1924, Palm Beach County sheriff George "Bob" Baker, John Ashley's old adversary, led a posse and ambushed the Ashley Gang's hideout. A shootout ensued, and Joe Ashley was killed. Also killed was Palm Beach County deputy sheriff Frederick "Fred" Baker. Laura Upthegrove was wounded in the melee but managed to slip away into the Everglades with the other surviving Ashley Gang members.

On September 12, 1924, the Ashley Gang stole $5,000 in cash and $18,000 in securities in an armed robbery of the Bank of Pompano. John Ashley gave an unspent bullet to the bank cashier and said, "You give that to Sheriff Bob and tell him I got another one just like it waitin' for him if he's man enough to come and get it." In response, Sheriff Baker boasted that he would one day claim John Ashley's glass eye as a trophy.

The feud between John Ashley and Sheriff Baker escalated to the point where Baker led a posse into the Everglades and destroyed anything they found that was believed to belong to the Ashley Gang. Sheriff Baker managed to smoke the Ashley Gang out of the Everglades. As the gang was preparing to relocate to Jacksonville, Francis Mario, husband of John Ashley's sister Lola, tipped off Stuart police chief Oren B. Padgett of the gang's plan. Chief Padgett knew the gang would be crossing over the Sebastian River Bridge and contacted Sheriff Baker, who then called St. Lucie County sheriff J.R.

THE TRUE STORY OF HOW FOUR OF THE ASHLEY GANG MEMBERS DIED

In the 1950s, Ada Coats Williams, instructor at Fort Pierce's Indian River Community College, was told the true story of the Sebastian River Bridge ambush by a retired deputy who was at the scene on November 4, 1924. All of the other law enforcement officers were dead by this time. The retired deputy revealed the true story: "Convinced that no jail could hold the gang, the deputies had determined to finish them off. They cuffed John Ashley and made him raise his hands. As they cuffed the others, Ashley began to drop his hands. A deputy shot him dead. The others fired wildly and the rest of the gang was killed." The four members of the Ashley Gang were murdered in cold blood by Florida law enforcement officers.

The bodies of John Ashley, Hanford Mobley, Clarence Middleton and Ray "Shorty" Lynn were taken to Fort Pierce. Since the Ashley Gang were infamous for their escapes and gunning down law enforcement officers, the public was skeptical that four of their members were killed. The next day, the mortuary in Fort Pierce displayed all four bodies on the sidewalk to prove to the public that four of the notorious Ashley Gang were dead. John Ashley's glass eye had been removed and given to Palm Beach County sheriff Baker.

The notorious Ashley Gang, circa 1925. *Clockwise, starting at top*: John Ashley, Hanford Mobley, Clarence Middleton, Roy "Young" Matthews, Ray Lynn. *Center*: John Ashley and his sweetheart, Laura Upthegrove, King and Queen of the Everglades. *Courtesy of State Archives of Florida.*

John Ashley's girlfriend, Laura Upthegrove, was furious and sent word to Sheriff Baker that stated, "If you don't put back that glass eye, I'll crawl through Hell on my hands and knees to kill you." Baker quickly returned John Ashley's glass eye in time for his burial at his family's plot in Gomez.

On December 5, 1928, Heywood Register, the last surviving member of the Ashley Gang, escaped from Raiford Penitentiary. Sheriff Baker and two deputies tracked him down along the Boynton Canal and killed him in a shootout on January 29, 1930.

Merritt to set up a trap. They decided to string a heavy chain over the Dixie Highway at the south side of the Sebastian River Bridge. Sheriff Baker sent Palm Beach County deputies Elmer Padgett, Henry Stubbs and L.B. Thomas to assist Sheriff Merritt and two of his St. Lucie County deputies. Sheriff Baker did not take part in the ambush plan.

Sheriff Merritt received word that members of the Ashley Gang were approaching the Sebastian River Bridge in a black Model-T Ford automobile. Around 10:30 p.m., under the cloak of darkness, a car pulled up to the bridge, and sheriff deputies approached with sawed-off shotguns, but it was two innocent civilians. Moments later, another car pulled up behind and stopped; it was four members of the Ashley Gang. The sheriff deputies quickly surprised the gang members before they were able to respond and arrested them.

Arrested were John Ashley, Hanford Mobley, Clarence Middleton and Ray "Shorty" Lynn. Ashley was handcuffed individually, and the other three were handcuffed together, as reported by Miller and Davis, the two men who were in the car in front of the Ashley Gang and witnesses to the arrest.

What happened next has always been controversial, as all four of the Ashley Gang members were shot to death by law enforcement. The *Tampa Bay Times* headline on November 4, 1924 was "Four Ashley Bandits Are Killed—Six Deputies and Merritt Escape without Injury during Gun Battle with Outlaws." Other newspaper accounts of the time reported similar stories that said the Ashley Gang attempted to escape and the lawmen had no choice but to shoot the gangsters dead in defense. A judge ruled the shootings were justifiable, and the officers involved took an oath of silence regarding the incident.

Federal Government Poisons Industrial Alcohol

Perhaps the most atrocious cause of deaths during Prohibition was the federal government's program of adding poisons to industrial alcohol products that were produced in the United States in an attempt to discourage people from drinking it. This is also referred to as the "chemist's war of Prohibition." The percentage of purity is the main difference between commercial-grade and industrial alcohol.

This program was prompted by the federal government's frustration that people were continuing to drink alcoholic beverages during Prohibition.

This was one of the deadliest and most irresponsible governmental programs in American history. It is estimated that at least ten thousand people died as a result of this governmental poisoning program during the years of Prohibition. One of the main problems was the ease with which industrial alcohol reached the public as it was resold as drinkable spirits.

During Prohibition, medical doctors became accustomed to treating patients for alcohol poisoning, as cheap bathtub gin, moonshine and watered-down liquor was often contaminated with various impurities, some very toxic. Some of this black-market alcohol was mixed with additives such as creosote (a mixture of chemicals that is a thick and oily flammable liquid), lead toxins and even embalming fluid. As a result, many people were sickened, paralyzed, blinded and even suffered painful deaths. Since the illegal liquor trade was unregulated, there were no governmental inspections to verify that alcoholic beverages distributed anywhere in the nation were safe. However, the flurry of hospitalizations and deaths due to people drinking industrial alcohol was surely concerning to both the public and medical doctors.

By the mid- to late 1920s, Prohibition enforcement was managing to slow the liquor smuggling from Canada, and the U.S. Coast Guard was stifling rumrunners from the Caribbean. Although illegal liquor smuggling was still a huge problem, criminal syndicates sought an easier method to supply alcoholic beverages by stealing huge quantities of industrial alcohol. By the mid-1920s, the U.S. Treasury Department estimated that around sixty million gallons of industrial alcohol was being stolen every year. Criminals hired chemists to redistill industrial alcohol into a drinkable liquid.

In 1926, President Calvin Coolidge ordered the manufacturers of industrial alcohol to add ingredients to make their products taste so bad that they would be unpalatable. By the end of 1927, there was an array of poisonous ingredients being mixed into industrial alcohol, including acetone, benzene, brucine, cadmium, camphor, carbolic acid, chloroform, ether, formaldehyde, gasoline, iodine, kerosene, mercury salts, nicotine, quinine and zinc. Government officials ordered more methyl alcohol be added, up to 10 percent of the total volume. This amount of methyl alcohol additive was the most lethal ingredient in industrial alcohol.

During the holiday season of 1926, 1,200 people were sickened by poisonous alcohol, and 400 died. In 1927, the number of reported deaths was around 700. Public health officials around the nation were alarmed and some outright furious at the federal government's poison industrial alcohol program.

Charles Norris, New York's first appointed chief medical examiner and pioneering forensic toxicologist, often said that the federal government's program of adding poisons to industrial alcohol was "our national experiment in extermination."

A January 18, 1927 article in the *Tampa Tribune* titled "Wanted—Something Nasty" states:

> *There are plenty of recipes for drinks in this Prohibition age. Now what is wanted is a recipe to prevent drinking. Uncle Sam's chemists so far have failed to provide one. There might be a national competition, with the Treasury Department or the Anti-Saloon League offering a prize.*
>
> *It is a question of making alcohol too nasty to drink, without making it deadly. The public doesn't approve of the government putting actual poison into commercial alcohol, because death is regarded as an unholy severe penalty for defying Prohibition. As long as there are people weak and foolish enough to drink liquids never intended for drinking, they must be protected against themselves.*

U.S. senator Edward Irving Edwards of New Jersey stated in December 1926 that the federal government was guilty of "legalized murder" because it mandated and allowed poisons to be mixed with industrial alcohol.

U.S. senator James Reed of Missouri became an outspoken critic of the federal government's industrial poison program, as he explained in December 1926:

> *The sole purpose of Prohibition was to protect the life, health and morals of the people, but when the government puts poison into alcohol, a large percentage of which the government knows will ultimately be consumed for beverage purposes, such action is reprehensible and tends to defeat the very purpose of Prohibition, namely, the conservation of life and health.*
>
> *Indeed, it seems to me that he who puts poison in any liquid food, knowingly at the time that a large percentage of the poisoned article will be consumed by people, has himself been guilty of a crime.*

Wayne Wheeler, of the Anti-Saloon League and the main lobbyist for the drys, announced that the victims of the federal government's poison industrial alcohol program were "deliberate suicides" and deserved no sympathy. Some of the most ardent supporters of Prohibition were appalled at Wheeler's heartlessness.

The federal government's poison industrial alcohol program continued until the repeal of Prohibition in 1933.

Chapter 9

NATIONAL PROHIBITION IS REPEALED

By the early 1930s, it was clear to most people that the "noble experiment" had failed miserably and had created many more problems than what was ever anticipated. Prohibition did not put an end to alcohol consumption; instead, it turned millions of otherwise law-abiding citizens into lawbreakers. It also increased unlawful and dangerous activities such as bootlegging, moonshining and rumrunning. With the nation bogged down in the Great Depression, organized crime flourishing, tax revenues stifled and a half million jobs dependent on reestablishing the liquor and beer brewing industries, it seemed the nation was anxious to repeal Prohibition.

FDR's Anti-Prohibition Campaign Strategy

In 1932, Democratic presidential candidate Franklin D. Roosevelt made it perfectly clear that the repeal of Prohibition was one of his priorities. In his August 27, 1932 campaign address in Sea Girt, New Jersey, FDR discussed the effects of alcohol abuse:

> *It is bound up with crime, with insanity and, only too often, with poverty. It is increasingly apparent that the intemperate use of intoxicants has no place in this new mechanized civilization of ours. In our industry, in our recreation, on our highways, a drunken man is more than an objectionable*

companion, he is a peril to the rest of us. The hand that controls the machinery of our factories, that holds the steering wheel of our automobiles, and the brains that guide the course of finance and industry, should alike be free from the effects of over-indulgence in alcohol.

FDR went on to state the failures of Prohibition and to advocate the repeal of the Eighteenth Amendment:

But the methods adopted since the World War with the purpose of achieving a greater temperance by the forcing of Prohibition have been accompanied in most parts of the country by complete and tragic failure. I need not point out to you that general encouragement of lawlessness has resulted; that corruption, hypocrisy, crime and disorder have emerged, and that instead of restricting, we have extended the spread of intemperance. This failure has come for this very good reason: we have depended too largely upon the power of governmental action instead of recognizing that the authority of the home and that of the churches in these matters is the fundamental force on which we must build. The recent recognition of this fact by the present Administration is an amazing piece of hindsight. There are others who have had foresight. A friend showed me recently an unpublished letter of Henry Clay, written a hundred years ago. In this letter Clay said that the movement for temperance "has done great good and will continue to do more" but "it will destroy itself whenever it resorts to coercion or mixes in the politics of the country."

We advocate the repeal of the Eighteenth Amendment. To effect such repeal, we demand that the Congress immediately propose a Constitutional Amendment to truly representative conventions in the States called to act solely on that proposal.

FDR surely gathered a lot of support from the wets for his anti-Prohibition stance, but other issues were top priorities as well, especially the tanking U.S. economy due to the Great Depression, which started on Black Tuesday (the Wall Street Crash of 1929). By 1932, almost a quarter of American workers were unemployed, many had lost their homes and farms and tens of thousands of people were wondering where their next meal would come from.

Florida's economic problems predated the Great Depression. The state had been experiencing a severe economic decline since 1926, when its short-lived economic prosperity of the Florida land boom went bust. By

"Do Your Bit—Repeal the Eighteenth Amendment—Elect Franklin D. Roosevelt President." Campaign poster with contribution pledge section, circa 1932. *Courtesy of Wikimedia Commons.*

1932, the state of Florida had the scarcest resources and greatest debt of any state in the country.

The United States was in dire need to be led out of the disastrous Prohibition era and had to find quick solutions to dig itself out of the Great Depression. The 1932 presidential election pitted the incumbent Republican candidate Herbert Hoover, who was perceived as the status quo, against the Democratic candidate FDR, who was perceived as a symbol of change and hope.

FDR won the 1932 presidential election in a landslide over Hoover. FDR secured 57.4 percent of the votes, while Hoover mustered 39.6 percent.

Florida's Support for FDR in 1932

Florida held its 1932 U.S. presidential election on November 8, 1932. The state had seven presidential electors for the Electoral College. At this time, Florida was virtually a one-party state with the Democratic Party dominant. There were a few Republican Party strongholds, including the growing urban areas of Orange and Pinellas Counties, in which Hoover received over 40 percent of the votes. FDR won Florida's 1932 presidential election in a landslide over Hoover. FDR secured 74.49 percent of the votes, while Hoover mustered 24.98 percent. All seven presidential electors were won by FDR.

THE CULLEN-HARRISON ACT

Within a few days after FDR took office as president of the United States, he kept his campaign promise to repeal Prohibition. The first thing on his agenda for the repeal of Prohibition was to ask Congress to hold a special session to modify the Volstead Act to legalize beer with an alcohol content of 3.2 percent (by weight) and wine of a low alcohol content.

On March 21, 1933, Congress enacted the Cullen-Harrison Act, which passed by large majorities in both the House and the Senate. The bill was sponsored by Representative Thomas H. Cullen of New York and Senator Pat Harrison of Mississippi.

The Florida delegation in the House overwhelmingly voted in favor of the Cullen-Harrison Act. Peterson of Lakeland, Green of Starke, Caldwell of Milton and Wilcox of West Palm Beach voted yes; Sears of Jacksonville was absent and did not vote.

FDR signed the bill on March 22, 1933, and it took effect on April 7, 1933, in the eighteen states and the District of Columbia, which had passed similar legislation. The federal law required each state to pass legislation to allow the sale of 3.2 percent beer and wine of low alcohol content.

"I think this would be a good time for a beer."
—President Franklin D. Roosevelt

Some breweries were working around the clock in the days before April 7, 1933, to have 3.2 percent beer ready. Thousands of people gathered around breweries, and an estimated 1.5 million barrels of beer was consumed on April 7.

The Cullen-Harrison Act was considered a win for FDR, as it not only led the charge to repeal Prohibition, but it also decreased unemployment by generating many jobs in the brewing industry and provided critical tax revenue for the government during the economic crisis of the Great Depression. The bill was expected to bring in $125 to $150 million in annual revenue for the federal government.

The Twenty-First Amendment

National Prohibition lasted for thirteen years, ten months and nineteen days, until it came to an end on December 5, 1933, when Utah became the thirty-sixth state (which was the decisive vote toward the three-fourths of the states required) to ratify the Twenty-First Amendment. Florida was the thirty-first state to ratify it, which occurred on November 2, 1933.

The passing of the Twenty-First Amendment marked the first, and only, time in American history that a constitutional amendment (the Eighteenth) was repealed.

About an hour after Utah's announcement, President Roosevelt issued a statement that declared the end of Prohibition. Roosevelt also asked that the

TAMPA MORNING TRIBUNE
40TH YEAR—NO. 340
TAMPA, FLORIDA, WEDNESDAY, DECEMBER 6, 1933
PRICE FIVE CENTS
THE ASSOCIATED PRESS
PROHIBITION WIPED OUT

"Prohibition Wiped Out," the page-one headline of the *Tampa Tribune* on December 6, 1933.

"What America needs now is a drink."
–President Franklin D. Roosevelt

people of the nation drink responsibly and not abuse alcoholic beverages in what he referred to as a "return of individual freedom."

On the day Prohibition was repealed, Yuengling Brewing Company, the nation's oldest brewery, located in Pottsville, Pennsylvania, delivered a special batch of "Winner Beer" to the White House for FDR's enjoyment.

Although the headline of the *Tampa Morning Tribute* on December 6, 1933, read "Prohibition Wiped Out," it was a little overly optimistic, as only eighteen states immediately became wet. Florida was one of thirty states that remained dry due to statewide alcohol prohibition laws. National Prohibition was certainly wiped out by the Twenty-First Amendment, but the wets still had a lot of work to do in Florida, and around the country, to get legal liquor flowing.

U.S. GOVERNMENT RUSHES LIQUOR CONTROL PLANS

President Roosevelt was concerned that the supply of liquor was low and many areas did not have adequate regulatory processes in place, so few liquor suppliers were operational. Roosevelt said, "The policy of the government will be to see to it that the social and political evils that existed in the pre-Prohibition era shall not be revived nor permitted again to exist." The regulatory plans were being rushed to prevent underworld bootleggers from taking advantage of the increased demand for liquor.

Joseph H. Choate Jr., head of the newly formed Federal Alcohol Control Administration, reported that one of his first priorities was to speed up the supplies of liquor around the nation. The Federal Alcohol Control Administration's temporary liquor import committee was busy issuing permits to import large quantities of American-type bourbon and rye whiskey.

At the state level, the main problem was with regulatory controls to manage legal liquor.

Many voices from the temperance movement were lobbying for a return to Prohibition. Edwin E. Blake, national secretary of the Prohibition Party, predicted that the United States would soon return to national Prohibition. Dr. Howard Hyde Russell, founder of the Anti-Saloon League, was

Twenty-First Amendment

Section 1.

The eighteenth article of amendment to the Constitution of the United States is hereby repealed.

Section 2.

The transportation or importation into any state, territory, or possession of the United States for delivery or use therein of intoxicating liquors, in violation of the laws thereof, is hereby prohibited.

Section 3.

This article shall be inoperative unless it shall have been ratified as an amendment to the Constitution by conventions in the several states, as provided in the Constitution, within seven years from the date of the submission hereof to the states by the Congress.

lobbying for new federal alcohol regulatory legislation. Many clergymen and bootleggers, not surprisingly, were in favor of returning to Prohibition.

At Least Thirteen Thousand Prohibition Offenders Go Free

On February 5, 1934, the U.S. Supreme Court ruled, in a unanimous decision, that approximately nine thousand cases involving at least thirteen thousand people charged with violating federal Prohibition laws, and not yet tried or who had been convicted and were pending an appeal, would go free.

The Supreme Court stated, "Upon the ratification of the 21st Amendment, the 18th Amendment at once became inoperative…The grant of authority to the Congress by the 18th Amendment, immediately fell with the withdrawal by the people of the essential constitutional support." The Supreme Court also stated, "The 21st Amendment contained no saving clause as to have effect on December 5, [1933] when the 21st Amendment was ratified."

The Supreme Court pointed out that the people themselves repealed the Eighteenth Amendment and said, "The principle involved is thus not archaic but rather is continuing and vital—that the people are free to withdraw the authority they have conferred, and when withdrawing, neither the Congress nor the court can assume the right to continue to exercise it."

This ruling did not affect pending state-level cases pertaining to violations of state prohibition laws. It also did not affect people who were convicted of violating federal Prohibition laws prior to the passing of the Twenty-First Amendment who were serving prison sentences.

The U.S. Justice Department said its policy, since the Twenty-First Amendment had passed, was to "give more favorable consideration to applications for pardons from those who had good records aside from their Prohibition violations than to those from racketeers and gangsters."

FLORIDA REPEALS ITS STATEWIDE PROHIBITION

On November 6, 1934, voters in Florida overwhelmingly voted to repeal the statewide prohibition of alcohol. The state went back to the previous system of local county option. A November 7, 1934 article titled "State Legalizes Liquor Selling with Restrictions—Florida Again Wet after Dry Spell of Some 16 Years" in the *Palm Beach Post* explains the system:

> *Under the terms of the repeal amendment approved by general election voters, citizens still cannot legally hang a foot on the rail and gulp a whiskey and soda, despite that it has been openly done in many sections of the state ever since national repeal went into effect.*
>
> *The new amendment specifies a return in Florida to the laws prevailing at the time bone-dry constitutional prohibition went into effect in 1919.*
>
> *The principal one of these statues is the Davis Package Law fixing the terms under which liquor stores may be operated in wet counties. All but four counties were dry under local option when prohibition went into effect.*

Beer and other low-alcohol content drinks were legal everywhere in the state, but dry counties (there were twenty-four in 1934, mostly in the conservative panhandle) prohibited the sale of liquor.

It took some states a lot longer than Florida to repeal their statewide prohibition. Kansas did so in 1948, and Mississippi was the last state to do so in 1966.

Chapter 10

ALCOHOL RESTRICTIONS IN FLORIDA AFTER NATIONAL PROHIBITION

After Prohibition was repealed by the Twenty-First Amendment, Florida passed legislation to allow legal beer to be sold around the state; however, the sales of liquor were left to each county. Florida laws required each county to hold two referendums when deciding liquor sales. One referendum question was the sale of liquor (going wet or dry), and the other was about liquor being sold in packages or as individual drinks. Some counties voted to stay dry, some went wet and others voted to allow liquor sales but only permitted packaged liquor sales from a retail store or prohibited individual drinks from being sold. These referendums were usually highly contested affairs, as the business community challenged the rural and religious citizenry of each county.

By the 1990s, only a scattering of counties was dry in Florida.

Davis Package Law

After Florida repealed its statewide prohibition of alcohol on November 6, 1934, the state used its antiquated Davis Package Law, which governed the sale of liquor prior to 1919. Under the Davis Package Law, liquor store owners paid $1,000 for a state and county license. There was no set amount that cities could charge for liquor store licenses. The law also disallowed the sale of liquor on Sundays, limited the sales of liquor to sealed containers and required liquor stores to close at nighttime.

This law was unpopular, as it caused confusion for liquor store owners, patrons and law enforcement. Several lawsuits were filed challenging the validity of the Davis Package Law. One particular lawsuit was filed by Earlish Sasser, operator of the Pig 'n' Pickle resort in Clearwater Beach. Lawyers claimed that when Sasser was arrested for selling liquor by the drink, law enforcement could not find that illegal because when the Florida statutes were revised in 1920, the Davis Package Law was not included. They went on to claim "that the statute could have been reenacted only by act of the legislature in due legislative form...Only the legislature can enact laws—the people can't."

On January 8, 1935, Judge T. Frank Hobson issued an informal opinion saying that the Davis Package Law was invalid, but he was waiting for a formal ruling by the Florida Supreme Court.

On January 19, 1935, Florida's Supreme Court ruled "that liquor statues in effect when [statewide] prohibition was voted in 1918 merely were 'laid at rest or in repose,' and that they immediately became operative again as soon as Prohibition was voted out of the Constitution."

Two liquor charges against Earlish Sasser were dismissed. Sasser purchased a state and county liquor license, and a cache of whiskey worth almost $1,000 seized during a May 5, 1935 sheriff's raid at the Pig 'n' Pickle resort was returned.

FLORIDA LIQUOR CONTROL LAW OF 1935

The 1935 Florida legislature passed a new Florida Liquor Control Law, and it was signed on May 27, 1935, by Florida governor David Sholtz. The law went into effect on June 26, 1935, and allowed the sale of alcohol by the drink in the state's forty-five wet counties. The law also included several other stipulations, including:

All liquor that was stored by retailers since Prohibition was repealed was now subject to state gallonage taxes.
All liquor bottles were required to have revenue stamps affixed to them.
All retailers were required to pay taxes on all liquor they sell.
Licensed liquor wholesalers could only sell to licensed liquor retailers.
Persons engaged in the enforcement of this law were prohibited from having any financial interest in the sale of liquor.
Wholesalers were prohibited from having any financial interest in any retail liquor establishment.

Wholesale and retail liquor license fees ranged from $200 annually in counties with less than a population of ten thousand to $750 annually in counties with a larger population. There were special liquor license fees for boats, clubs and trains.

Each county and city with liquor establishments could levy taxes equal to 50 percent of the state tax.

Liquor manufacturers were required to pay license fees from $50 to $1,250 annually.

The sale of liquor on Sundays was banned if the liquor establishment was within 2,500 feet of a church or school in rural areas of the state.

Municipalities were given the right to regulate the hours of liquor sales and the location of liquor establishments within their city limits.

Liquor taxes imposed by the state were eighty cents per gallon on liquor; fifty cents per gallon on champagne; ten cents per gallon on wine made in the state; and six cents per gallon on beer, which was already in effect. The retail price for liquor immediately rose around the state as retailers added around twenty cents a quart, or ten cents a pint, to every bottle they sold.

The state expected to collect about $2,500,000 annually from fees for dealer liquor licenses and taxes on liquor, wine and beer.

Blue Laws

Historically, blue laws in the United States were written to enforce the Christian Sabbath (a day reserved for rest and worship). They were also referred to as "Sunday laws" or "Sunday closing laws." Blue laws were restrictive by design and tended to ban certain activities, mainly the sales of specific goods or services on a certain day, or days, of the week.

Blue laws were mostly in effect during the colonial era (a period that lasted from the early seventeenth century to the late eighteenth century). After the late eighteenth century, blue laws that banned common tasks such as housework and travel were mostly disregarded. However, some blue laws were observed to prevent working on Sundays and to ban or limit the use of alcoholic beverages.

In the United States, blue laws were resurrected in the late nineteenth and early twentieth centuries by the temperance movement to limit or ban the use of alcoholic beverages.

The U.S. Supreme Court has upheld some blue laws, such as a day of rest for mail carriers. At the state level, some blue laws restrict the sale of alcoholic beverages on Sundays.

DRY COUNTIES IN FLORIDA

As of 2023, Liberty County is the only completely dry county in Florida. Lafayette County is partially dry, as it limits sales of alcohol to packages, and alcohol above 6.243 percent cannot be sold. Alcohol sales are limited to weekdays.

In 2022, Washington County was dry until 66 percent of the voters were in favor of going wet. The county now allows the sale of packaged liquor and individual alcoholic beverages to be sold in bars and restaurants.

Before 2012, Madison County was partially dry, as it prohibited the sale of packaged liquor. In 2012, voters in Madison County repealed that law. However, in unincorporated sections of the county, the sale of packaged alcoholic beverages is still prohibited on Sundays.

In 2011, Suwanee County was dry until voters approved the sale of liquor (67.5 percent) and the sale of packages and individual drinks (73.1 percent).

In 1951, Leon County, home to Florida's state capital Tallahassee, voted to stay dry. In 1960, voters allowed sales of liquor but prohibited individual drinks from being sold. In 1967, Leon County voted for the sale of liquor (73.1 percent) and the sale of liquor packages and individual drinks (65.9 percent). It took a while, but the state capital of Florida was finally wet.

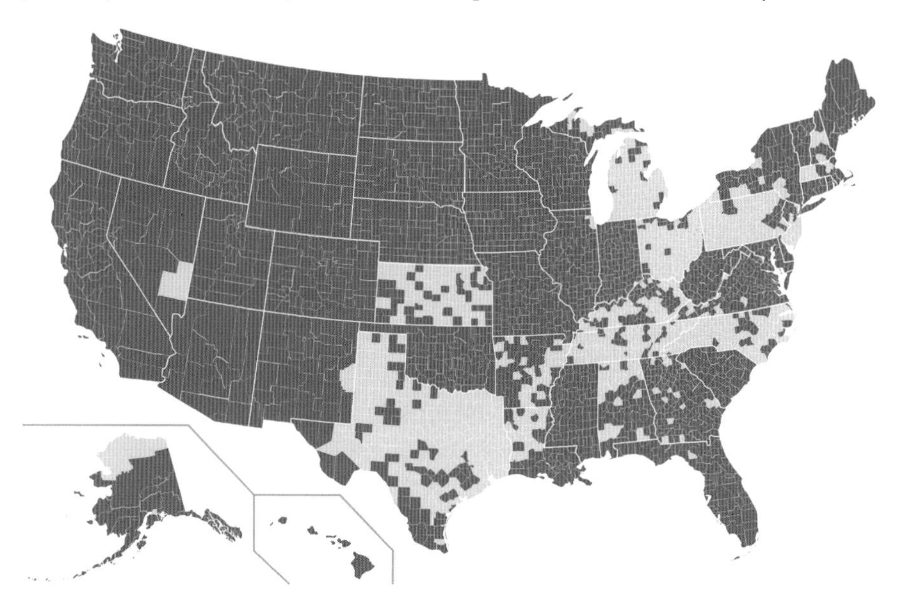

Map showing dry (*light gray*), wet and mixed (*dark gray*) counties, parishes and boroughs in the United States as of May 2019. *Courtesy of Wikimedia Commons.*

Current Alcohol Laws in Florida

Current alcohol laws in Florida are different from county to county due to local laws. Beer, wine and liqueurs (alcoholic beverages bottled with added sugar and flavors derived from fruits, herbs or nuts) are sold in convenience and retail stores and supermarkets. Liquors or spirits are sold in retail package liquor stores.

Florida alcohol laws include:

- A person must be twenty-one years or older to purchase and consume alcoholic beverages.
- A person may not sell, furnish or serve alcoholic beverages to anyone under twenty-one years of age or allow a person under twenty-one to consume alcoholic beverages on licensed premises.
- A person must be eighteen years of age to serve alcoholic beverages.
- A person must be twenty-one years of age to pour alcoholic beverages.
- A person must be eighteen years of age to sell packaged liquor.
- If an establishment has sales from food that make up 50 percent of their total sales, minors under eighteen years of age are allowed inside. Minors can sit at the bar as long as they are not consuming alcoholic beverages.
- Establishments typically do not sell alcoholic beverages between 3:00 a.m. and 7:00 a.m. (except for passengers traveling in railroad cars).
- The days and hours of alcoholic beverage sales are primarily under the jurisdiction of local counties and cities. Miami-Dade County is one of the few counties that allow the sale of alcoholic beverages twenty-four hours, seven days a week.
- Drinking alcoholic beverages on public property such as streets, sidewalks, parking lots and beaches is prohibited.
- Drinking alcoholic beverages on private property is prohibited if the owner has not given permission.
- State law does not prohibit the sale of alcoholic beverages on Sundays; however, many counties allow sales, and many have restrictions that limit the hours for sales.

- Retailers such as grocery and convenience stores can begin selling beer and wine, for off-site consumption, at 10:00 a.m. on Sundays.
- Retailers are prohibited from selling liquor on Sundays, unless a specific county has approved it through a referendum.

Florida also has some substantial penalties for violating alcohol laws. Penalties include: prison for sixty days and a fine of $500 for purchasing alcoholic beverages under the age of twenty-one; and prison for up to five years and a fine up to $5,000 for using fake identification to purchase, or attempt to purchase, alcoholic beverages.

Some have said it was easier to obtain alcoholic beverages in Florida during Prohibition than it is today.

Current Florida State Taxes on Alcohol

State taxes on alcohol in Florida are some of the highest in the United States. In Florida, the primary taxes on alcohol are placed on beer, wine and liquor (which includes most types of hard alcohol, or hard liquor, which are distilled alcoholic beverages).

- Taxes on beer in Florida are ranked seventh highest in the United States.
    - Beer vendors pay $0.48 per gallon.
    - Florida's general sales tax for beer is 6 percent of the purchase price.
- Taxes on wine in Florida are ranked second highest in the United States.
    - Wine vendors pay $2.25 per gallon, $3.00 per gallon over 17.259 percent and $3.50 per gallon for sparkling wine.
    - Florida's general sales tax for wine is 6 percent of the purchase price.
- Taxes on liquor in Florida are ranked fourth highest in the United States.
    - Liquor vendors pay $2.25 per gallon under 17.259 percent, $6.50 per gallon between 17.260 percent and 55.779 percent and $9.53 per gallon over 55.780 percent.
    - Florida's general sales tax for liquor is 6 percent of the purchase price.

Chapter 11

PROHIBITION'S LEGACY

Most people believe that Prohibition was a dismal failure for many reasons. At least half the population wanted to drink alcohol at the onset of Prohibition, and tens of thousands, especially women, began drinking because it was the trendy thing to do. Prohibition's enforcement was riddled with failures, contradictions, corruption, hypocrisy and defiance at all levels of law enforcement agencies and within the ranks of governmental officials. Prohibition outlawed personal freedoms, expanded federal law enforcement powers, bankrolled organized crime, eliminated tens of thousands of jobs, reduced tax revenue and created opportunities for bootleggers and moonshiners to make and distribute tons of unregulated alcoholic beverages, some toxic and poisonous, which was obviously harmful to society.

During Prohibition, a few beneficial things did happen, including a reduction in arrests for public drunkenness, a drop in alcohol consumption (especially in the beginning), empowerment for women and the modernization of the U.S. Coast Guard.

Complete and accurate statistics on the consumption of alcohol during Prohibition are nonexistent. Estimates were derived by using data on arrests for public drunkenness, deaths caused by cirrhosis of the liver, deaths caused by alcoholism and hospital admittance records for alcoholic psychosis. All of these statistics point to a sharp drop in alcohol consumption in the beginning of Prohibition to approximately 30 percent of the pre-Prohibition level. By the mid-1920s, alcohol consumption was on the rise. Interestingly, alcohol consumption remained almost the same immediately following the repeal of Prohibition as it did during the last years of Prohibition.

In the 1920s and 1930s, increasing numbers of women entered the workforce, gained the right to vote via the Nineteenth Amendment (mostly White, as the majority of Black women were disenfranchised due to poll taxes, threats and literacy tests), enjoyed new mass consumer culture and urbanism, smoked cigarettes, drank alcohol and danced in jazz clubs, which equates to the gaining of more personal freedoms.

The U.S. Coast Guard's largest law enforcement mission ever was the enforcement of Prohibition. This U.S. military service branch experienced significant growth during Prohibition in both personnel and ships. Aviation, intelligence gathering, personnel training and radio communications were all greatly improved. The aviation branch became permanent, U.S. Coast Guard crews manned navy warships and the Coast Guard Intelligence Office was established. All of these improvements and expansion significantly prepared the U.S. Coast Guard for World War II.

Prohibition's legacy includes an increase of legal restrictions on the sale of alcoholic beverages and large tax revenues collected by local, state and federal governmental agencies. In 1934, the first year after repeal, the federal government collected more than $258 million in alcohol taxes. This accounted for almost 9 percent of the government's tax revenue for 1934. Taxes on alcohol continued to benefit the federal government in the ensuing years. Some of this money was used to support crucial New Deal initiatives (a series of programs and projects that were aimed at restoring the nation's economy by creating jobs and offering relief to suffering people during the Great Depression).

Obviously, Prohibition did not stop people from drinking alcoholic beverages. Today, Americans are drinking an average of 2.3 gallons of pure alcohol per year, approximately twelve standard drinks per week. This means that Americans are drinking the same amount of alcohol as compared to pre-Prohibition levels.

Now, more than ninety years after the repeal of Prohibition, many believe that the major lesson learned is that bans on personal freedoms rarely, if ever, work in a democratic society.

Appendix I

FLORIDA'S FIVE GOVERNORS DURING THE PROHIBITION ERA

Sidney Johnston Catts (1863–1936)—served as Florida's twenty-second governor from January 2, 1917, to January 4, 1921, as a member of the Prohibition Party.

Sidney Johnston Catts was born on a plantation in Pleasant Hill, Alabama. His father, Samuel W. Catts, was a captain in the army of the Confederate States of America.

In 1882, Catts earned a law degree from the Cumberland School of Law. From 1885 to 1910, he was an ordained pastor in Alabama. In 1910, he moved to Florida and worked as an insurance salesman and a preacher sermonizing temperance, anti-Catholicism, family values and moral improvement.

In 1914, Catts announced he would run for the Florida governor's seat as a member of the Democratic Party. Catts became the first Florida governor's candidate to travel in an automobile on the campaign trail. He visited and campaigned in many rural and remote areas where some of the residents had never seen an automobile before. He had no political experience and was a new resident of the state, anti-Catholic, a staunch prohibitionist and a racist.

Catts's anti-Catholic viewpoints were unfounded in Florida, as the state's Catholics made up only about 5 percent of the population in 1915. The main concern for anti-Catholics at the time was the large numbers of Catholic immigrants who were coming into the United States in the early twentieth century. Catts said, "There is no question that rum and Romanism go together."

The June 1916 Florida Democratic gubernatorial primary election included candidates Sidney Catts, Florida treasurer William B. Knott, former Speaker of the House Ian Ferris and Frank A. Wood, a banker and former state legislator from St. Petersburg.

The novice Catts was initially declared the winner, but Knott demanded a runoff. The Florida Supreme Court declared Knott the winner by a very narrow margin after four months of political maneuvering. Knott entered the 1916 Florida gubernatorial general election as the Democratic Party candidate. Catts, the Democratic Party's outsider and malcontent, decided less than a month before the election to run as the Prohibition Party candidate. George W. Allen ran as the Republican Party candidate.

As Catts campaigned around Florida, a rumor spread that Apalachicola Catholics were planning to assassinate him. Catts began brandishing two loaded pistols, which added to his mystique as a maverick.

On November 7, 1916, the Florida gubernatorial election was held. Sidney Catts won with 47.71 percent of the vote, William Knott finished second with 36.61 percent and George Allen finished a distant third with only 12.47 percent.

For the first, and only, time in U.S. history, a Prohibition Party candidate won a gubernatorial election. The *New York Times* referred to Catts's improbable upset as "spectacular."

On January 2, 1917, Catts was sworn in as Florida's twenty-second governor. He refused to attend his own inaugural ball because he was opposed to dancing.

Catts proposed a Florida state income tax and the taxation of church property and urged the support of women's suffrage. He also promoted free student textbooks and a statewide good roads movement. He was appalled at the state's practice of using convict laborers, something he experienced firsthand in west Florida. He persuaded Florida legislators to abolish this cruel practice.

In 1919, a strike of three thousand phosphate workers in Polk County pitted wealthy businessmen against Catts. Ironically, many of the workers were Black, and Catts was a known bigot. The mining companies sent hundreds of Black replacement workers. This caused violence, as an automobile was ambushed, killing a strikebreaker and wounding a deputy sheriff. A group of guards opened fire in the town of Mulberry and killed three Black people. Catts removed Polk County sheriff John Logan because he felt he did not do enough to prevent the violence.

In 1920, Catts was ineligible to run for the Florida governor's seat due to term limits. Instead, he ran for the U.S. Senate but was walloped by incumbent Democratic senator Duncan U. Fletcher by a 2–1 margin.

The Florida Senate investigated Catts for supposed bribes, unethical pardons and appointments and the involuntary servitude of two Black people whom he allegedly forced to work on his plantation. He was eventually acquitted on all charges.

In 1924 and 1928, Catts ran for the Florida governor's Democratic nomination but lost in both primary elections.

In 1928, he was among the few Democrats who supported Republican Herbert Hoover for president of the United States over Democrat Al Smith, a Catholic.

On March 9, 1936, Catts died in DeFuniak Springs, Florida, at the age of seventy-two.

Cary A. Hardee (1876–1957)—served as Florida's twenty-third governor from January 4, 1921, to January 6, 1925, as a member of the Democratic Party.

Cary A. Hardee was born on November 13, 1876, in Taylor County, Florida. In 1900, he was admitted to Florida's bar and began a career as a lawyer. Prior to his legal career, he was an educator. Hardee also had a successful banking career where he established two banks: the First National Bank of Live Oak (eventually becoming its president) and the Mayo State Bank. He was also the president of the Branford State Bank.

In 1905, Hardee became Florida's Third Judicial District's state attorney. He began his political career in the Florida House of Representatives, serving from 1915 to 1919. He was elected as the Speaker of the Florida House for both of his terms.

In 1920, Hardee ran for governor of Florida with a campaign strategy of creating a better and more efficient state government. An article in the *St. Lucie County Tribune* on January 16, 1920, stated that "[Hardee is]…the openly avowed champion of better Government in Florida—and candidly and fearlessly states exactly where he stands on the leading issues in the Gubernatorial Campaign."

In the 1920 Florida gubernatorial election, Hardee won with 103,407 votes, which was an overwhelming 77.94 percent.

In addition to dealing with Prohibition, Hardee's term oversaw the establishment of six new counties, started the first state tax on gasoline, stopped leasing state prisoners to private businesses and established electrocution as a legal method of execution.

In March 1921, Hardee ordered the re-arrest of Harry S. Black, a New York multimillionaire who was arrested for violation of Prohibition laws and then released by United States commissioner John M. Graham. William Jennings Bryan (three-time Democratic Party candidate for president of the United States and national Prohibition supporter) sent Hardee the following telegram: "The Tourist's Bible Class of the First Presbyterian church, numbering 2,000, has read with great satisfaction your telegram to Sheriff Allen, ordering strict enforcement of state prohibition law, regardless of action of federal officials, and by unanimous vote heartily commends your course. Strength to your arm." Many Florida residents, especially Prohibition supporters, were impressed with Hardee's determination to prosecute a multimillionaire in defiance of a federal official's decision.

Hardee offered to send the National Guard to assist with the infamous Rosewood Massacre incident (a racially motivated massacre of at least six Black people, and two white people, and the destruction of the Black town of Rosewood by large groups of white aggressors in January 1923). However, Levy County sheriff Robert Elias Walker declined the National Guard assistance.

In 1925, Hardee retired from the Florida governor's office after one term. He ran again in 1932 but lost in the Democratic primary, coming in third behind David Sholtz and John W. Martin.

Hardee resumed his banking career and died in Live Oak, Florida, on November 21, 1957. Florida's Hardee County is named in his honor.

JOHN WELLBORN MARTIN (1884–1958)—served as Florida's twenty-fourth governor from January 6, 1925, to January 8, 1929, as a member of the Democratic Party.

John W. Martin was born on June 21, 1884, in Plainfield, Florida. He was admitted to the Florida bar in 1914. He became mayor of Jacksonville in 1917 at age thirty-two (the city's youngest mayor). He served three consecutive terms and then decided to run for the Florida governor's seat.

In 1924, Martin defeated former Florida governor Sidney Catts in the Democratic primary. He went on to defeat Republican William R.

O'Neal by a margin of 65.58 percent of the votes in the 1924 Florida gubernatorial election.

Martin County was established on May 30, 1925, named after Governor John Martin while he was in office. Martin spearheaded road and highway development and the construction of an industrial plant for physically disabled Florida prisoners. He also obtained financing for public schools by direct state appropriations and supplied free textbooks to all students through the sixth grade.

The Florida land boom was in full swing when Martin took office, but it collapsed during his tenure, causing economic turmoil around the state. Two of Florida's most historic and horrific hurricanes—the 1926 Miami and the 1928 Okeechobee—killed almost three thousand people and devastated portions of the state. Martin attempted to obtain financing to build safer docks and re-engineer drainage along Lake Okeechobee. These projects were part of the Rivers and Harbors Act of 1930 but started after Martin's tenure as governor of Florida.

Martin left the Florida governor's office on January 8, 1929. He ran for the United States senator's seat against incumbent Park Trammel in 1928 but lost in the Democratic primary election. In 1932, Martin ran for the Florida governor's seat again but was defeated by a wide margin in a runoff Democratic primary election against David Sholtz.

Martin eventually made his way back to Jacksonville, where he practiced law. He and former senator Scott Loftin were appointed co-trustees of the Florida East Coast Railway.

Martin died on February 22, 1958, in St. Augustine.

Doyle Elam Carlton (1885–1972)—served as Florida's twenty-fifth governor from January 8, 1929, to January 3, 1933, as a member of the Democratic Party.

Doyle E. Carlton was born on July 6, 1885, in Wauchula, Florida. In 1912, he earned an LLB degree from Columbia University and was admitted to the Florida bar and began practicing law in Tampa.

In 1916, Carlton was elected to the Florida Senate, where he represented the Eleventh District (Hillsborough and Pinellas Counties).

From 1925 to 1927, he served as the city attorney of Tampa.

In 1928, there were five candidates in the Democratic Party gubernatorial primary: Doyle E. Carlton; Sidney Johnston Catts, former Florida governor;

Fons A. Hathaway, chairman of the Florida State Road Department; John Stansel Taylor; and J.M. Carson. Carlton won with 77,569 votes (30.24 percent). The Florida gubernatorial election was held on November 6, 1928. Carlton ran against the Republican Party candidate, William J. Howey, mayor of Howey-in-the-Hills. Carlton won with 148,455 votes (60.97 percent). In his inaugural address, Carlton said, "Simplicity in state government, with abolition of useless offices and economy in the operation of all departments will be the aim…for the next four years."

The Great Depression took center stage during Carlton's administration. He cut many state jobs and cut his own salary to reduce the state's budget. He initiated a three-cent sales tax on gasoline to maintain and construct new highways. In 1931, Carlton's veto of the bill to legalize pari-mutuel betting was overridden due to the need for more state revenue.

In 1936, after leaving the Florida governor's office, Carlton ran for the U.S. Senate but lost to Charles O. Andrews, former state representative from Orlando, in the Democratic Party primary election.

In December 1957, President Dwight D. Eisenhower appointed Carlton to the Commission on Civil Rights, where he served until 1961.

In 1961, Carlton was appointed to the National Agricultural Advisory Commission, where he served until 1963.

On October 25, 1972, Carlton died in Tampa at the age of eighty-seven.

David Sholtz (1891–1953)—served as Florida's twenty-sixth governor from January 3, 1933, to January 5, 1937, as a member of the Democratic Party.

David Sholtz was born on October 6, 1891, in Brooklyn, New York. In 1914, Sholtz earned a law degree from Stetson University Law School and began practicing law in Daytona Beach.

In 1917, Sholtz was elected to the Florida House of Representatives but resigned from his seat to serve in the U.S. Navy during World War 1.

From 1919 to 1921, he served as a state attorney for the Seventh Judicial Circuit, and in 1921, he became the city judge of Daytona Beach.

From 1928 to 1929, he was the president of the Florida Chamber of Commerce.

In 1932, Sholtz entered the gubernatorial campaign with very little funding and was considered a long shot. Many of his campaign speeches were conducted from a flatbed truck with two mounted loudspeakers. His campaign platform strongly favored education, as he advocated free school textbooks, back pay for teachers and a nine-month school year. Other issues he supported included an increase of government services, public welfare and banking regulations.

One of Sholtz's opponents, former governor John W. Martin, used anti-Semitic attacks against him even though he was an active member of the Episcopal church in Daytona Beach.

On June 7, 1932, the Florida Democratic primary election included seven candidates, and Sholtz finished in second place, which was a surprise as he knocked former governor Cary A. Hardee out of the runoff. In the runoff, a bigger surprise emerged as Sholtz defeated former governor John W. Martin and became the Democratic candidate for the Florida governor's seat. In the general election of 1932, Sholtz won against the Republican candidate, William J. Howey, receiving 66.62 percent of the votes.

Sholtz, a friend of President Roosevelt, was part of the New Deal coalition and supported New Deal policies. During his administration, he established the Florida Citrus Commission and the Florida Park Service and followed through with the passing of a workmen's compensation bill.

Sholtz was also a supporter of states voting on the issue of Prohibition. On February 21, 1933, he said, "Congress has submitted the whole question of Prohibition repeal to states which is the right and proper course provided by the federal constitution. The issue now becomes one for the individual states. It is my desire that the people of Florida have an opportunity to vote upon the whole question of state and federal Prohibition with unnecessary delay. I shall recommend to the legislature that these questions be submitted to the electorate of Florida in prescribed manner."

Sholtz's tenure experienced the end to national Prohibition on December 5, 1933, and the end of Florida's state prohibition on November 6, 1934.

After Sholtz left the Florida's governor seat, he ran for the U.S. Senate in 1938. He lost to Claude Pepper in the Florida Democratic primary.

On March 21, 1951, Sholtz died in Key West at the age of sixty-one.

Appendix II

THE FIVE U.S. PRESIDENTS DURING THE PROHIBITION ERA

Woodrow Wilson (1856–1924)—served as the twenty-eighth president of the United States from March 4, 1913, to March 4, 1921, as a member of the Democratic Party.

Woodrow Wilson was born on December 28, 1856, in Staunton, Virginia. He experienced the ravages of the American Civil War firsthand as his family moved around the South during his youth. Wilson earned several college degrees. He started out at Davidson College. In 1875, he transferred to the College of New Jersey (now Princeton). He then pursued a law degree at the University of Virginia and a PhD in political science at Johns Hopkins University.

Wilson's academic teaching career started at Bryn Mawr and Wesleyan. In 1890, he became a professor at the College of New Jersey. In 1902, he became the university's president and spearheaded new and innovative curriculum advancements. During Wilson's tenure, the College of New Jersey became the prestigious Princeton University.

In 1910, Wilson was elected governor of New Jersey as an inexperienced, untested and unconventional candidate. He served from January 17, 1911, to March 1, 1913.

Progressives in the Democratic Party convinced Wilson, a determined reformer, resolved scholar and ardent orator, to seek the party's nomination for president of the United States in the 1912 election. Wilson used his New Freedom platform (progressive programs), which assisted his campaign to victory over incumbent Republican president William Howard Taft and the Progressive or "Bull Moose" candidate Theodore Roosevelt. The third party run by Roosevelt wound up splitting the Republican Party votes and actually assisted Wilson to victory. Wilson was able to pass laws that benefited small businesses, farmers and the average American. In 1913, the Underwood-Simmons Act reduced tax rates for small businesses. Also in 1913, the Federal Reserve Act allowed the average American access to more loans. In 1914, the Clayton Antitrust Act supported labor unions by allowing boycotts, peaceful picketing and strikes.

On July 26, 1914, World War I broke out in Europe. Wilson declared that the United States would remain neutral during this global conflict. As World War I raged, Germany ignored the neutrality of the United States and sank American ships. Wilson finally asked Congress to declare war in April 1917.

The participation of the United States boosted the strength of the Allies, which led to victory against the Central Powers. World War I ended on November 11, 1918. Wilson's proposed "Fourteen Points" was a guideline for a peace treaty. It included the creation of the League of Nations (the precursor to the United Nations). In 1920, Wilson was awarded the Nobel Peace Prize.

On October 27, 1919, Wilson vetoed the Volstead Act because it included the enforcement of wartime prohibition (this act banned the sale of alcoholic beverages with an alcohol content greater than 1.28 percent, which was intended to allocate grain to the war effort). Congress overrode his veto the next day.

As the women's suffrage movement continued to grow, Wilson became a supporter. Wilson joined his daughter, Jessie Woodrow Wilson Sayre, and contacted members of Congress to ask for their support. On August 18, 1920, the Nineteenth Amendment was ratified, which finally gave women the right to vote.

Wilson was a bigot and racist. When he was president of Princeton University, he wrote that eastern and southern Europeans are "men of the lowest class." Wilson also praised the 1915 silent film *The Birth of a Nation*, which condemned Reconstruction and prompted the rise of the Ku Klux Klan.

Wilson appointed several southern Democrats to his cabinet. They spearheaded a number of racist Jim Crow policies that segregated federal employment. These Jim Crow policies segregated bathrooms and cafeterias and made some federal buildings "white only." In November 1914, Wilson told civil rights leader William Monroe Trotter that "segregation is not a humiliation but a benefit, and ought to be so regarded by you gentlemen."

Wilson's first wife, Ellen Louise Axson, died of kidney disease in 1914. On December 18, 1915, he married Edith Bolling Galt and quickly entrusted her with affairs of the president's office. In October 1919, Wilson suffered a stroke, and Edith stepped in behind the scenes to make many decisions on his behalf. In fact, many historians believe that Edith acted as the first female president of the United States. Wilson did make a partial recovery from his stroke but remained disabled for the rest of his life.

Woodrow Wilson died on February 3, 1924, in Washington, D.C., at the age of sixty-seven.

Warren G. Harding (1865–1923)—served as the twenty-ninth president of the United States from March 4, 1921, to August 2, 1923, as a member of the Republican Party.

Warren G. Harding was born on November 2, 1865, in Corsica, Ohio (now Blooming Grove). Harding entered the Ohio Central College at age fourteen. He became editor of the college's newspaper and excelled at public speaking. In 1882, he graduated and went to work as a teacher in a country school and sold insurance. He teamed up with two friends to purchase the failing *Marion Daily Star* newspaper in Marion, Ohio. The publication continued to struggle under their ownership but did eventually become successful.

In 1898, Harding's wife, Florence Mabel Kling Wilson, convinced him to pursue political office. He was elected that same year to the Ohio legislature and served two terms.

In 1903, he became lieutenant governor of Ohio, serving two years. Afterward, he returned to the newspaper business.

In 1910, he ran for the Ohio governor's seat but lost the election.

Harding won the election for the U.S. senator's office in 1914. He served from March 4, 1915, to January 13, 1921.

At the Republican Party's national convention in June 1920, Harding became the presidential nominee. Harding used the campaign slogan "Return to Normalcy." Harding won the presidential election with 60.4 percent of the vote and carried thirty-seven of forty-eight states in the Electoral College.

Harding's administration set out to reverse much of the progressive legislation that had been passed over the previous twenty years. Tax cuts on higher incomes, protective tariffs, limitations on immigration and enhanced civil liberties for Black people were all championed by Harding.

Some of Harding's high-level appointees known as the "Ohio Gang" caused problems and bred corruption, which unleashed several scandals. One of the most problematic incidents was the Teapot Dome Scandal. Harding's secretary of the interior, Albert B. Fall, leased oil-rich lands in Wyoming to various companies that provided him personal loans. In 1931, Fall was sentenced to prison for corruption.

Harding and his wife hosted many garden parties and state dinners at the White House where they served plenty of liquor in violation of several Prohibition laws.

In an attempt to repair his reputation, Harding and his wife took a political trip to the western part of the nation. While returning from Alaska, Harding became sick and was rushed to a hospital in San Francisco, California. On August 2, 1923, Harding died in San Francisco, while in office, from a massive heart attack at the age of fifty-seven.

After Harding's death, one of his extramarital affairs with Nan Britton was exposed. Britton wrote a book and claimed Harding had fathered her daughter. This caused a media sensation and launched a feud between the Harding and Britton families.

In 2015, DNA testing proved that Nan Britton's daughter, Elizabeth Ann Blaesing, was the biological daughter of Harding.

Calvin Coolidge (1872–1933)—served as the thirtieth president of the United States from August 2, 1923, to March 4, 1929, as a member of the Republican Party.

On July 4, 1872, Calvin Coolidge was born in Plymouth Notch, Vermont. Coolidge attended Amherst College in Amherst, Massachusetts. In 1897, he did a law apprenticeship at a firm in Northampton, Massachusetts, and was admitted to the bar. In 1898, he started his own law practice.

In 1898, Coolidge started his political career as a city councilman in Northampton, Massachusetts. He went on to hold the offices of city solicitor and clerk of courts.

In 1906, Coolidge was elected to the Massachusetts House of Representatives. He also served as the mayor of Northampton and as a state senator of Massachusetts.

In 1915, he was elected as the forty-sixth lieutenant governor of Massachusetts, and in 1918, he was elected as the forty-eighth governor of Massachusetts.

In 1920, he was elected the twenty-ninth vice president of the United States under President Warren Harding. Coolidge was the first vice president to attend cabinet meetings.

On August 2, 1923, President Harding died while in office. Coolidge, the vice president and legal successor to the president's office, was away from the nation's capital visiting his family in Vermont. The Coolidge family home did not have electricity or a telephone, so he was informed of Harding's death by a messenger. His father, John Calvin Coolidge Sr., who was a notary public, actually swore Coolidge in as the thirtieth president of the United States.

President Coolidge did not support most regulations except tariffs and did not support foreign alliances. He signed the Indian Citizenship Act, which granted full U.S. citizenship to all Native Americans. He approved of civil rights and appointed Black people to government jobs and refused to appoint any known associates of the Ku Klux Klan. Coolidge did not support the United States joining the League of Nations and did not recognize the Soviet Union as a nation.

Coolidge was commended for his attitude on Prohibition. A September 14, 1923 article in the *Times Recorder* stated:

> *Whole hearted commendation of the attitude of President Coolidge on Prohibition was expressed in a meeting here today of the executive committee of the Anti-Saloon League of America. Attorney General Daugherty was given praise for the report which he made to President Coolidge and for what the executive committee denominated a determination to make a drastic enforcement of the Volstead Act.*

In 1924, Coolidge was nominated by the Republican Party for president of the United States. He ran against John W. Davis, the Democratic candidate, and Robert M. La Follette, the Progressive Party candidate. Coolidge won with 54 percent of the vote.

In 1927, Coolidge announced that he would not seek a second full term as president of the United States. His statement simply said, "I do not choose to run for President in 1928."

Calvin Coolidge died on January 5, 1933, in Northampton, Massachusetts at the age of sixty.

Herbert Hoover (1874–1964)—served as the thirty-first president of the United States from March 4, 1929, to March 4, 1933, as a member of the Republican Party.

Herbert Hoover was born on August 10, 1874, in West Branch, Iowa. Hoover attended Stanford University and graduated in 1895. He became a prominent mining engineer and published the book *Principles of Mining* in 1909, which became a standard textbook.

At the beginning of World War I, while the United States was considered neutral, Hoover established the Commission for Relief in Belgium. This organization distributed over two million tons of food to nine million victims of war.

When the United States entered World War I in April 1917, President Wilson appointed Hoover as head of the U.S. Food Administration. This organization managed the food needs for the United States during the war.

After World War I ended, Europe was left in dire need of food supplies. The U.S. Food Administration changed to the American Relief Administration. Hoover was now managing food supplies for central and eastern Europe. Hoover's reputation as a humanitarian emerged from his World War I hunger-relief efforts.

In 1920, Hoover was appointed secretary of commerce by President Harding. He served in that capacity from 1920 through 1928, which spanned the Harding and Coolidge administrations.

In 1927, when President Coolidge announced he would not seek reelection, Hoover quickly became the front-runner and did receive the nomination for the Republican Party's presidential candidate.

On November 6, 1928, Hoover defeated the Democratic Party's candidate, Al Smith, as he received 58.2 percent of the votes.

Hoover's famous campaign statement was, "We in America today are nearer to the final triumph over poverty than ever before in the history of any land." Nothing could have been further from the truth, as the stock market crashed in 1929 and ushered in the Great Depression, the worst economic crisis in the nation's history.

Hoover tried several programs to restore the economy, including the urging of businesses to not implement wage cuts or start layoffs; the establishment of the Reconstruction Finance Corporation (a lending institution to help banks and industries recover); tax cuts; and public works projects. He also signed the disastrous Smoot-Hawley Act, which raised taxes on imports and reduced the amount of exported domestic goods. This act actually worsened the economic conditions of the Great Depression. All of Hoover's efforts to combat the Great Depression fell short of expectations as tens of thousands of people lost jobs and became poverty stricken.

Hoover turned against national Prohibition during his presidency, and while on his reelection campaign, he made it quite clear, to the dismay of the wets. An article in the *Buffalo Evening News* on August 13, 1932, discusses Hoover's stance:

> *The presidential campaign Saturday had gone into a new phase, with President Hoover's turn against national Prohibition clearing the air, starting political realignment on a broad front and bringing a flood of telegraphic support from all parts of the country.*
>
> *With Republican wets quite generally accepting the President's stand for state liquor control as satisfactory the political spotlight turned on the organized dry forces. It found them bewildered by the suddenness of Mr. Hoover's decision to abandon the 18th Amendment as a failure, while insisting on saloon suppression.*

The presidential election of 1932 pitted the incumbent Republican Hoover against the Democratic candidate Franklin D. Roosevelt. Hoover's failure to effectively battle the Great Depression surely played a role in his crushing defeat. Roosevelt received 57.4 percent of the votes compared to Hoover's 39.6 percent.

Herbert Hoover died on October 20, 1964, in New York City at the age of ninety.

FRANKLIN DELANO ROOSEVELT (1882–1945)—served as the thirty-second president of the United States from March 4, 1933, to April 12, 1945, as a member of the Democratic Party.

Franklin D. Roosevelt was born on January 30, 1882, in Hyde Park, New York. He was an only child of a wealthy family. Until age fourteen, Roosevelt was educated by private tutors and governesses.

In 1896, Roosevelt enrolled at the Groton School for boys, a private college-preparatory boarding school in Groton, Massachusetts. He graduated in 1900 and then enrolled at Harvard University. In 1903, Roosevelt graduated with an AB degree in history.

In 1904, Roosevelt entered the Columbia Law School. He passed the New York bar examination in 1907 and subsequently dropped out of Columbia. In 1908, he was hired at the well-respected law firm of Carter Ledyard & Milburn in New York City.

In 1910, Roosevelt began his political career by winning a seat in the New York state senate. In 1912, he was reelected and served as chairman of the agricultural committee, where he supported farm, labor and social welfare bills.

Roosevelt supported Woodrow Wilson for the presidential candidate at the 1912 Democratic Convention in Baltimore. After Woodrow Wilson was elected president of the United States, he appointed Roosevelt as assistant secretary of the navy in 1913. Roosevelt served in this role for more than seven years. He supported a large and modernized naval force, founded the U.S. Navy Reserve and learned the valuable lessons of labor issues, naval procedures and wartime logistics from his World War I experience.

In 1914, Roosevelt ran for a New York U.S. Senate seat but was defeated in the Democratic primary election.

In 1920, he accepted the vice presidential nomination at the Democratic National Convention in San Francisco. James M. Cox was his running mate as the presidential candidate. Roosevelt and Cox were soundly defeated in the 1920 presidential election by Warren Harding (president) and Calvin Coolidge (vice president).

In 1921, Roosevelt was diagnosed with polio and became permanently paralyzed. He thought his political career was over, but his wife, Eleanor, and political advisor, Louis Howe, convinced him to pursue a life in politics.

In 1928, Roosevelt was elected as governor of New York. His progressive political agenda led to several new social programs.

When the nation fell into the Great Depression in 1929, Roosevelt began preparing for a run for president by advocating governmental intervention for economic relief, recovery and reform programs. He also promised the repeal of national Prohibition.

In the presidential election of 1932, Roosevelt soundly defeated incumbent Herbert Hoover. Roosevelt received 57.4 percent of the vote compared to Hoover's 39.6 percent.

President Roosevelt's position on Prohibition was spelled out in a June 5, 1933 article in the *Bristol Herald Courier*:

> *President Roosevelt is against National Prohibition. He opposed its adoption because he does not believe in sumptuary laws or that the Government*

should undertake to say what the individual shall eat or drink. He favors its repeal because he is convinced that it has failed to accomplish its purpose, that National Prohibition has produced evils as great as those that existed in the days of the saloon, and that the best solution of the liquor problem is legalized traffic under a system of regulation and control in which the saloon shall have no part.

On December 5, 1933, Prohibition was repealed by the Twenty-First Amendment. President Roosevelt wasted no time in announcing the end of Prohibition to the nation.

Roosevelt created the New Deal within the first one hundred days after taking the president's office. The New Deal expanded the power of the national government and brought enormous economic reforms throughout the nation during the recovery from the Great Depression.

Roosevelt served an unprecedented four terms as president of the United States. He led the nation out of the Great Depression and through most of World War II.

Franklin D. Roosevelt died on April 12, 1945, while in office, in Warm Springs, Georgia, at the age of sixty-three.

Roosevelt's presidency during World War II propelled the United States into a superpower on the world stage.

Appendix III

THE TEMPERANCE MOVEMENT AND PROHIBITION-ERA COMIC POSTCARDS

Postcards are an excellent way to get a pictorial glimpse into the cultural, societal and political climate of a particular time in history. The study and collection of postcards is called deltiology. Postcards are an inexpensive, mass-produced means of communication that were especially popular during the nineteenth and twentieth centuries. Postcards are sometimes the only known surviving pictorial record of an event, street scene, people, landscape, waterway, building or other man-made device or machine, which oftentimes makes them an important historical artifact.

During the temperance movement and the Prohibition era, postcards depicted the battle between the drys and wets. The postcards included in the following collection all have a comical anecdote. However, they conveyed captivating messages that either supported the public use of alcoholic beverages or projected anti-alcohol sentiments.

All postcards date from the period of around 1900 to 1933 and are from the author's collection.

"Attention Ladies and Gentlemen—This Country Needs a Good 5 Cent Glass of Beer."

"Drinking Again, Eh?"

"How we miss you! How things have changed since John Barleycorn died."

"I just Fell Off the Water-Wagon."

"If you are all in—how much are you out?"

"Prohibition Has Sent Many a Fine Man to the Jug—Ye Village Jug."

"I'm Sitting Up and Taking Nourishment. How Are You Getting On?"

"Say—Who's Your Bootlegger?"

"The Spirits of Today—Moonshine—Wood Alcohol, Poison, Jakey [Jamaica Ginger]."

"U.S. Bone Dry—We're on the Water-Wagon but I Am Better Off!"

BIBLIOGRAPHY

Alcohol Problems and Solutions. "Alcohol in Colonial America: Earliest Beginnings." alcoholproblemsandsolutions.org/alcohol-in-colonial-america-earliest-beginnings-in-the-new-world.

Alduino, Frank. "The Damnedest Town This Side of Hell: Tampa 1920–29 (Part 1)." *Sunland Tribune* 16 (1990), article 6.

Behr, Edward. *Prohibition: Thirteen Years that Changed America*. New York: Arcade Publishing, 2011.

Blumenthal, Karen. *Bootleg: Murder, Moonshine, and the Lawless Years of Prohibition*. New York: Roaring Brook Press, 2011.

Bristol Herald Courier. "Roosevelt and Prohibition." June 5, 1933.

Buffalo Evening News. "Drys Bewildered at Hoover's Stand." August 13, 1932.

Bureau of Alcohol, Tobacco, Firearms and Explosives. "James E. Bowdoin." www.atf.gov/our-history/fallen-agents/james-e-bowdoin.

Burns, Ken, and Lynn Novick, dirs. *Prohibition*. Arlington, VA: Public Broadcasting Service (PBS), 2011.

Carter, James A., III. "Florida and Rum Running during National Prohibition." *Florida Historical Quarterly* 48, no. 1 (July 1969): 47–56.

Casetext. *Buchanan v. State*. February 22, 1928. casetext.com/case/buchanan-v-state-69.

Cooke, Bill. "Sixty Years Before the Cocaine Cowboys, Miami Was the Wild West of Prohibition." *Miami New Times*, February 23, 2016.

Crary, David. "100 Years Later, Prohibition's Legacy Remains." *PBS News Hour*, January 14, 2020. www.pbs.org/newshour/arts/100-years-later-prohibition-legacy-remains.

Evening Herald. "Bootlegger's Murdered Remains Found in Shack Near Miami; Is Third Alleged 'Runner' Killed." January 9, 1925.

———. "Was Ashley Gang that Attempted to Arrange Miami Jail Delivery." September 28, 1925.

Flagler Tribune. "Klan Funeral for G.W. Durrance Held Last Sunday." September 1, 1927.

———. "Sheriff Perry Hall Killed by Negro Bootlegger at Roy." August 25, 1927.

———. "Ship Wrecked 5 Miles above Flagler Beach." December 3, 1925.

———. "Son Durrance in Shooting Affray Loses His Life." August 25, 1927.

Florida Department of State. "Cary Augustus Hardee." www.dos.myflorida.com/florida-facts/florida-history/florida-governors/cary-augustus-hardee.

———. "David Sholtz." www.dos.myflorida.com/florida-facts/florida-history/florida-governors/david-sholtz.

———. "Doyle Elam Carlton." www.dos.myflorida/florida-facts/florida-history/florida-governors/doyle-elam-carlton.

———. "John Wellborn Martin." www.dos.myflorida.com/florida-facts/florida-history/florida-governors/john-wellborn-martin.

———. "Sidney Johnston Catts." dos.myflorida.com/florida-facts/florida-history/florida-governors/sidney-johnson-catts.

Flynn, Meagan. "The 'Father of Prohibition,' Andrew Volstead, Didn't Volunteer for the Job. But He Got Years of Hate Mail for It." *Washington Post*, January 16, 2020.

Fort Lauderdale News. "Sheriff Bryan Jurors Fail to Agree as to Verdict." July 9, 1929.

Frazier, Brionne. "Eliot Ness: The Agent Who Brought Down Al Capone." ThoughtCo. December 31, 2018. www.thoughtco.com/elliott-ness-biography-4176371.

Guthrie, John J., Jr. "Hard Times, Hard Liquor, and Hard Luck: Selective Enforcement of Prohibition in North Florida, 1928–1933." *Florida Historical Quarterly* 72, no. 4 (April 1994): 435–52.

Jaye, Randy. *Flagler County, Florida: A Centennial History*. St. Petersburg, FL: Booklocker.com, 2017.

Jensen, Tom. "Birth of NASCAR Came 75 Years Ago." NASCAR Hall of Fame. December 14, 2022. www.nascarhall.com/blog/birth-of-nascar-came-75-years-ago.

Kleinberg, Eliot. "South Florida's Most Wily Gangster: John Ashley." *Palm Beach Post*, August 16, 2016.

Kobler, John. *Capone: The Life and World of Al Capone*. New York: G.P. Putnam's Sons, 1971.

Ling, Sally J. *Run the Rum In: South Florida during Prohibition*. Charleston, SC: The History Press, 2007.

McIntosh, Matthew A. "A History of Alcoholic Drinks Since the Ancient World." Brewminate, August 26, 2021. brewminate.com/a-history-of-alcoholic-drinks-since-the-ancient-world.

Miami Herald. "Bill for Beer Passes House by 316 to 97." March 15, 1933.

———. "Bryan's Class of 2,000 Backs Hardee Action in Black Case." March 21, 1921.

———. "Deputy Sheriff Shot to Death by Mistake." August 26, 1927.

———. "Federal Agents See Hinson Tote [Arrest Small-Time Moonshiner]." August 7, 1932.

———. "Indian River County Sheriff Joel Knight Took Bribes Grand Jury Charges." October 22, 1927.

———. "Sheriff Monroe Drowned When Boat Burns." March 26, 1921.

———. "Smell May Know but the Courts Say No—Smell of Mash Is Not Probable Cause to Warrant a Raid." November 2, 1932.

———. "Son of Old Man Ashley Was Killed During Battle at Dade County Jail." January 10, 1924.

The Miami News. "Captures an Enormous Moonshine Still at West Palm Beach." June 9, 1921.

———. "Carrie Nation Addressed the Public of Miami on Prohibition and Made a Decided Impression." March 10, 1908.

———. "Deaths Blamed on Liquor Code." December 31, 1923.

———. "Dry Enforcement Change Suggested—Woodcock Urges Aim at Commercial Violators." December 8, 1932.

———. "Florida to War on Rum Runners with Seaplanes." April 16, 1926.

———. "Letter to Coast Guard's Chief Warns of Deaths." August 27, 1927.

———. "Rehearing Denied Moore as Killer." June 4, 1932.

———. "State to Probe Killing of Two Liquor Agents [in West Palm Beach]." January 20, 1930.

———. "Ward Murder Arrest Made." July 1, 1926.

———. "Washington Man Discovers a War among Bootleggers; Miami Is Seat of Conflict." May 17, 1922.

Milanich, Jerald T., and Susan Milbrath. *First Encounters: Spanish Explorers in the Caribbean and the United States, 1492–1570*. Gainesville: University of Florida Press, 1989.

Miron, Jeffrey A., and Jeffrey Zwiebel. "Alcohol Consumption During Prohibition. National Bureau of Economic Research." Working Paper No. 3675, April 1991. www.nber.org/system/files/working_papers/w3675/w3675.pdf.

Morning Post. "Sen. James Reed Joins Attack on Poison Alcohol." December 31, 1926.

Morris, Allen C. "Five Hi-Jacker Bands Operate—Liquor Pirates Divide Miami Area into Districts for Mutual Benefit." *Miami News*, October 7, 1931.

News Press. "Florida Negro Shot in Georgia." September 12, 1927.

———. "Liquor Possession Cause of Big Fine." July 2, 1931.

Newton, Michael. *The Invisible Empire: The Ku Klux Klan in Florida*. Gainesville: University Press of Florida, 2001.

Officer Down Memorial Page. "Constable Arthur Fleece Crenshaw." www.odmp.org/officer/3610-constable-arthur-fleece-crenshaw.

———. "Federal Prohibition Agent James Edmund Bowdoin." www.odmp.org/officer/2088-federal-prohibition-agent-james-edmund-bowdoin.

———. "Federal Prohibition Agent John Van Waters." www.odmp.org/officer/13878-federal-prohibition-agent-john-van-waters.

Okrent, Daniel. "Wayne B. Wheeler: The Man Who Turned Off the Taps." Smithsonianmag, May 2010. www.smithsonianmag.com/history/wayne-b-wheeler-the-man-who-turned-off-the-taps-14783512.

Orlando Sentinel. "Raid on King of the Negro Bootleggers' Home Nets Twelve Gallons of Liquor." June 19, 1926.

———. "South Jacksonville City Heads Named in Rum Plot." May 18, 1928.

———. "T. Dennis 'King of the Negro Bootleggers' Sentenced to 60 Days in Jail." July 17, 1928.

Palm Beach Post. "Dry Agent's New Worry [Cow Shoes]." July 21, 1924.

———. "Nation Bone Dry after Midnight." January 16, 1920.

———. "Officers Convicted of Liquor Charges—South Jacksonville Authorities Found Guilty of Conspiracy." June 27, 1930.

———. "State Legalizes Liquor Selling with Restrictions—Florida Again Wet after Dry Spell of Some 16 Years." November 7, 1934.

Pensacola News Journal. "Aged Couple's Fate in Hands of High Court." March 17, 1928.

———. "Alderman Tells of Killing Two after Threats." January 25, 1928.

———. "Alleged Liquor Dealers Raided About Key West." February 17, 1926.

———. "Beer Raiders Launch Their Summer Drive." June 3, 1928.

———. "Dry Agents Nab Four and Seize Auto and Still." October 15, 1929.

———. "Officers Drying Up This Area." October 20, 1929.

Piket, Casey. "Al Capone in Miami." Miami History—The Magic City, May 18, 2015. miami-history.com/al-capone-in-miami-part-1-of-4.

Procko, Melissa. "The Way We Were: Bootleggers' Paradise: Orlando during the Prohibition Years." The Community Paper, January 28, 2021. www.yourcommunitypaper.com/articles/bootleggers-paradise-orlando-during-the-prohibition-years.

Pryor, Bailey, dir. *The Real McCoy: The Legend of Bill McCoy and the Rum War at Sea*. Mystic, CT: Telemark Films, Inc., 2007.

Rogers, David. "During Prohibition, Palm Beach Didn't Stay 'Dry.'" *Palm Beach Daily News*, December 8, 2013.

Sales Tax Handbook. "Florida: Alcohol Excise Taxes." www.salestaxhandbook.com/florida/alcohol.

Shalby, Colleen. "7 Things You Didn't Know about Alcohol in America." PBS, August 11, 2015. www.pbs.org/newshour/arts/7-things-didnt-know-alcohol-america.

Silvestri, Victor R., ed. *Encyclopedia of Florida Sheriffs 1821–2008*. Vols. 1–2. Clanton, AL: Heritage Publishing Consultants, Inc., 2008.

Soergel, Matt. "Bootleggers Were Big Business in the Woods and Swamps of Northeast Florida, in Prohibition and Beyond." *Florida Times-Union*, March 1, 2023.

St. Lucie County Tribune. "Cary A. Hardee Leading Candidate for Governor." January 16, 1920.

Storch, Gerald. "Our Cleo—The Bahama Queen—Memoirs of a Rum Runner." *Detroit Free Press*, June 13, 1965.

Tallahassee Democrat, "Posses Search for Slayer of Sheriff Hall." August 22, 1927.

Tampa Bay Times. "Former Leader of Wets Jumps to Dry Forces." January 29, 1920.

———. "Four Ashley Bandits Are Killed." November 2, 1924.
———. "Indian River County Sheriff Joel Knight Is Sent to U.S. Prison for Violation of Prohibition Laws." May 18, 1928.
———. "Is Tobacco Doomed?" May 21, 1921.
———. "Queen of Negro Bootleggers Is Re-Arrested." December 25, 1921.
———. "Sasser's Test of Liquor Law Ended by Ruling—Validity of Davis Package Law Upheld." January 23, 1935.
Tampa Times. "Boy Accused of Blasting Still Held—What Moonshine Did to a House." June 27, 1927.
———. "Officers Locate Big Moonshine Factory." April 26, 1930.
———. "U.S. Officials Rush Liquor Control Plans—Seek to Prevent Return of Evils of Pre-Prohibition." December 6, 1933.
———. "Yard Irrigated with Moonshine [in Jacksonville]." March 22, 1921.
Tampa Tribune. "Ancient Dream of the Dry Is a Fact Now." January 17, 1920.
———. "Booze Deaths." February 27, 1924.
———. "Bullet-Riddled Body of Negro Informer Is Found in River." March 26, 1926.
———. "Florida Dry Law Will Be a Dry One." November 28, 1918.
———. "Get Moonshine Still in Heart of the City." February 13, 1920.
———. "Moonshiner Killed in Battle with Officers." May 1, 1920.
———. "13,000 to Go Free on Dry Law Charges Court Rules." February 6, 1934.
———. "U.S. Jury Deadlocked in Miami Liquor Case—Sheriff Paul Bryan of Broward County." December 7, 1928.
———. "Wanted—Something Nasty." January 18, 1927.
———. "White Robed Figures Raid Negro Shiners." May 8, 1924.
Tasker, Fred. "Despite Prohibition, Liquor Flowed Here." *Miami Herald*, April 5, 2008.
Times Recorder. "Anti-Saloon League Approves Coolidge's Prohibition Views." September 14, 1923.
TIPS (Training for Intervention Procedures). "Blue Laws by State: What Are Sunday Blue Laws?" www.gettips.com/blog/sunday-blue-laws.
Vazquez, Christina. "Al Capone's Miami Beach Home Is No More—Here's Why the City Couldn't Save It from Demolition." Local10.com, August 11, 2023. www.local10.com/news/local/2023/08/11/al-capones-miami-beach-home-is-no-more-heres-why-the-city-couldnt-save-it-from-demolition.

Webb, Alice Jones. "How NASCAR Was Born of Bootlegging and Daredevils." Free Range American, February 16, 2023. freerangeamerican.us/bootlegging-roots-of-nascar/#:~:text=Bootlegging%20Roots%20of%20NASCAR&text=Even%20before%20Prohibition%20was%20repealed,crowds%20all%20through%20the%20South.

WestPalmBeach.com. "The Ashley Gang—West Palm Beach History." www.westpalmbeach.com/the-ashley-gang.

Zagorsky, Jay. "Prohibition's Legacy on American Drinking Today." *Kitsap Sun*, January 15, 2020. www.kitsapsun.com/story/opinion/columnists/2020/01/15/prohibitions-legacy-american-drinking-today/4480327002.

Zeitlin, Matthew. "Almost 90 Years after Prohibition, Some Places Are Still Dry. Why Is That?—How Prohibition Lives On in Counties across the Nation." Vox, December 17, 2019. www.vox.com/the-highlight/2019/12/7/20995187/prohibition-dry-county-alcohol-law-us.

ABOUT THE AUTHOR

Randy Jaye has had a lifelong interest in and passion for history. He has done extensive travel visiting, researching and photographing historic sites, museums and historical societies. He believes that studying history helps people understand how past events have shaped the present. He is also a firm believer that understanding the lessons of history can prevent undesirable events in our past from occurring again. He recently researched and nominated four properties that have been successfully added to the National Register of Historic Places. He is the author of three recent history books and writes articles for historical journals, local newspapers and magazines and has appeared on several radio shows and PBS documentaries. He earned both a Master's degree and a Bachelor's degree from California State University.